Green up your Cleanup

CREATIVE
HOMEOWNER®

Green up your Cleanup

JILL POTVIN SCHOFF

CREATIVE HOMEOWNER®, Upper Saddle River, New Jersey

Green Up Your Cleanup
Produced by Home & Garden Editorial Services
Project Manager: Joe Provey
Contributors: Roy Barnhart, Nicholas Day
Design: Horst Weber
Copy Editor: Owen Lockwood
Editorial Assistant: MaryAnn Kopp
Illustrations: Bob La Pointe
Front Cover Photography: Joe Provey, Home & Garden Editorial Services
Back Cover Photography: Joe Provey, Home & Garden Editorial Services

Creative Homeowner
VP, Publisher: Timothy O. Bakke
Production Director: Kimberly H. Vivas
Art Director: David Geer
Managing Editor: Fran Donegan
Senior Editor: Kathie Robitz
Photo Coordinator: Robyn Poplasky
Editorial Assistant: Nora Grace
Digital Imaging Specialist: Frank Dyer

Green Up Your Cleanup, First Edition
Library of Congress Control Number: 2007933864
ISBN-10: 1-58011-395-8
ISBN-13: 978-1-58011-395-3
Current Printing (last digit)
10 9 8 7 6 5 4 3 2 1

Printed in the United States of America

CREATIVE HOMEOWNER®
A Division of Federal Marketing Corp.
24 Park Way
Upper Saddle River, NJ 07458
www.creativehomeowner.com

Mixed Sources

Product group from well-managed forests, controlled sources and recycled wood or fiber
www.fsc.org Cert no. SCS-COC-00648
© 1996 Forest Stewardship Council

FSC

Dedication

For Rowan, who inspires me every day to work harder and do more.

Acknowledgments

Thanks to my husband for keeping the home fires burning while I slaved away on my laptop. And to Joe Provey and Owen Lockwood for always being such a pleasure to work with. Thanks to Dr. Robert Goodman, Ph.D., for his chemistry expertise and his willingness to answer a gazillion questions. And thanks to all of the members of various Internet forums where I've lurked and learned so much about green cleaning and what works and what doesn't. Very special thanks to A.J. Lumsdaine at solveeczema.org, who helped us finally find the cause of my son's eczema.

INTRODUCTION 10

Part I **THE BASICS**

CHAPTER 1
Why Go Green?   16
Making Changes 18
The Health Effect 20
The Environmental Impact 25
What You Can Do 30

CHAPTER 2
Your New Cleaning Arsenal 32
Cleaner By Cleaner 34
Tools of the Trade 46

Part II **INSIDE JOBS**

CHAPTER 3
The Fresh Bathroom   54
Showers and Tubs 56
Mold and Mildew 62
Toilets 70
Clearing Drains 72

contents

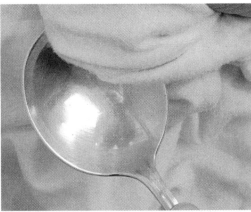

CHAPTER 4
Kitchen Detox 74
Sinks and Countertops **76**
Cabinetry **84**
Kitchen Appliances **85**
Kitchenware **86**

CHAPTER 5
Laundry You Can Live With 92
Eco Washing Strategies **94**
Eco Drying Strategies **96**
Eco Clothing Care **97**
The Green Alternatives **98**
Stain Guidelines **104**

CHAPTER 6
Around the House 106
Making Windows Sparkle **108**
Walls and Ceilings **112**
Cleaning Metal **120**
Dusting **122**

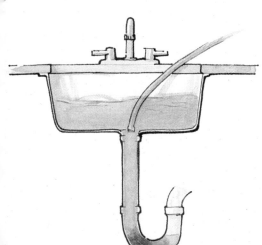

CHAPTER 7
All About Floors   126
Keep Out the Dirt **128**
Hardwood, Laminate, Bamboo,
  and Linoleum **132**
Tile, Stone, Rubber, Vinyl, and
  Concrete **134**
Rug and Carpet Care **138**

CHAPTER 8
Caring for Furnishings   146
Wood Furniture **148**
Other Hard Furniture **153**
Upholstery **155**
Window Treatments **159**

Part III DIRTY JOBS

CHAPTER 9
Outside the House   164
Vinyl, Aluminum, and Wood
  Siding **166**
Masonry **168**
Roofing **171**

Exterior Metalwork **175**
Decks **178**
Driveways, Walkways, and Patios **186**
Outdoor Furniture and Fabrics **188**
The Backyard Grill **190**

CHAPTER 10
Garage, Workshop,
and Basement   192
Garage Floors **194**
Cars **195**
Workshop Tools **200**
Paint Problems **202**
Lawn Mowers **205**
Pesticides **207**
Basements **208**

APPENDIX 212
RESOURCES 218
GLOSSARY 230
INDEX 234
PHOTO CREDITS 238

We live in a world that has its share of environmental problems, and we all want to be part of the solution. Perhaps you do your part to lead a green life by using compact fluorescent lightbulbs in your home. You may recycle your daily newspaper. Perhaps you walk or bicycle to the office each workday. But what about green cleaning?

My personal reasons for going green are outlined in Chapter 1. If you or other family members need additional convincing to switch to green cleaning, proceed to the Appendix on page 212. It details many of the hazardous chemicals you probably have under your sink and provides an array of health reasons for getting rid of them. If you're already convinced and just want to

Introduction

dive right in and get started, skip ahead to Chapter 2 and begin cleaning!

Inside you'll find plenty of information on making your own cleaners using simple recipes. I encourage you to give it a try. It's fun—and much easier than it sounds. You'll also find advice about store-bought products that are safe and work well. (See Resources for a complete list of companies that make eco-friendly products worth checking out.)

Part II of *Green Up Your Cleanup* starts with the two rooms you probably spend the most time cleaning: the bathroom and the kitchen. After that, we move to the laundry room, where I share some ecological washing strategies and provide green alternatives for getting rid of stains.

Next, I take you around the rest of the house, sharing green-cleaning insight about floors, ceilings, and everything in between them.

I tackle dirt where it lives in Part III. The final two chapters of the book cover all the cleaning jobs that you might encounter outside the house. I show you how to green clean everything from the deck and driveway to the garage and grill.

So sit back, relax (with a cup of green tea, perhaps?), and enjoy *Green Up Your Cleanup*. Don't forget that switching to green cleaning is a process and that it doesn't have to happen all at once. Take it at your own pace and just focus on making steady progress. Your family and the earth will be better off with every small step you take.

THE BASICS Part I

CHAPTER 1

Why Go Green?

My journey down the road to green cleaning started just three years ago. Before that I was like everyone else, buying the same cleaners off the shelf at the supermarket that my mom had used. I have always been a big supporter of the environmental movement, but somehow cleaning products just seemed so incidental that I had never gotten around to changing my habits.

All of that started to change when I got pregnant. I started focusing on articles about "body burden" and skyrocketing asthma and autism rates. The articles convinced me that my baby needed a home as chemical-free as possible. I started slowly, getting rid of what I knew to be toxic and looking for products at the store that said "nontoxic" and "all-natural." We chose low-VOC paint and natural wood furniture for the nursery, along with an organic mattress.

The big reason author Jill Schoff, left, became a green cleaning expert is the effect that commercial cleaners have on her son, right.

I was pretty satisfied with the state of our home when my son was born. But then at about 2 months old he got eczema. His skin was itchy and red and bleeding wherever he scratched it. We searched for months trying to figure out what was causing it. We finally stumbled onto a Web site called solveeczema.org. It suggested he might have a sensitivity to detergents—not just laundry detergents but all detergent products, including shampoo, dish soap, hand soap, and of course, most cleaning products—and that we should try switching to traditional soap products. We made the switch and it was really a miracle: my son's rash disappeared.

What I never realized is that the cleaning products we use now are almost all based on a relatively new type of surfactant (cleaning agent) developed during World War II. For simplicity's sake, throughout the book I will refer to these new surfactants as "detergents;" I will refer to the old-fashioned surfactants used for centuries as "soaps." Detergents work better in cold water, produce much less soap scum, and are cheaper to manufacture. For these reasons, traditional soap-based cleaners have almost disappeared from the marketplace.

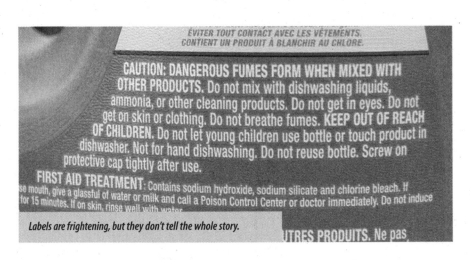

EVITER TOUT CONTACT AVEC LES VÊTEMENTS. CONTIENT UN PRODUIT À BLANCHIR AU CHLORE.

CAUTION: DANGEROUS FUMES FORM WHEN MIXED WITH OTHER PRODUCTS. Do not mix with dishwashing liquids, ammonia, or other cleaning products. Do not get in eyes. Do not get on skin or clothing. Do not breathe fumes. KEEP OUT OF REACH OF CHILDREN. Do not let young children use bottle or touch product in dishwasher. Not for hand dishwashing. Do not reuse bottle. Screw on protective cap tightly after use.

FIRST AID TREATMENT: Contains sodium hydroxide, sodium silicate and chlorine bleach. If se mouth, give a glassful of water or milk and call a Poison Control Center or doctor immediately. Do not induce for 15 minutes. If on skin, rinse well with water.

Labels are frightening, but they don't tell the whole story.

UTRES PRODUITS. Ne pas

Why Make the Switch?

If you've picked up this book, you probably have a general idea of the reasons behind green cleaning. In a nutshell, green means better for you, and better for the planet. Sounds good, but change is hard. Especially today when so many of us are so busy. It's easy to fall back on what is familiar because it's one less thing to think about.

Nevertheless, there are some strong reasons for switching to non-toxic cleaning methods, and I'm going to explain why making changes can do a tremendous amount of good for your family and for the earth. The most compelling of these reasons is that there is almost no government regulation of the chemicals used in cleaning products in the United States.

In this chapter, you will read about the harm that some of these chemicals are already doing. When you're done reading, I think you'll feel as I do: this change is essential for your family's health. The good news is that *there is no hardship or sacrifice involved*. Nontoxic cleaners really work—they clean better, they smell better, AND they save you money.

Unfortunately, detergents are not as wonderful we as originally thought. The main issue is that they compromise skin-barrier function. In other words, they make your skin more permeable, which allows more chemicals from the environment to make it through your skin and into your body. This is what caused my son's eczema, and it may account for increased asthma rates.

It was my search for detergent substitutes that forced me to truly become a green-cleaning expert. When pregnant, I had heard about cleaning with things such as baking soda and vine- gar, but I had discounted them, figuring there was no way something that simple could really clean. But when I realized that even plant-oil-based detergents could affect my son, I was forced to reconsider homemade recipes. (While far better for the environment, plant-based detergents function like any detergent and can open the door to health problems for some individuals.) And that's when my eyes were truly opened. You really can clean your home with simple ingredients. I've been cleaning my house without detergents for 2 years and I don't miss them.

In this book, you'll see the word "toxic" a lot. It's a strong word, conjuring images of hazardous waste and poison. I feel it's the right word to use. Merriam-Webster defines "toxic" as "containing or being poisonous material especially when capable of causing death or serious debilitation." It's shocking to think about it, but many of the ingredients in cleaning products are capable of this level of harm.

I know you're thinking that if certain

Where Are the Laws?

Currently in the United States there is almost no regulation of chemicals used in the home. (The only exception is pesticides.) According to a comprehensive review of the laws by the Environmental Working Group, chemical manufacturers are not required to perform any health or safety studies prior to the marketing and sale of a chemical; are not required to do any monitoring of chemicals once they are in use; and are allowed to claim virtually all information related to a chemical as confidential business information and thus forever shield it from government and public review.

The Toxic Substances Control Act is the main law regulating chemicals, and it's notorious for its protection of manufacturers. It prevents the Environmental Protection Agency (EPA) from requesting any data or health studies for a chemical unless the EPA can already demonstrate that a substance poses a significant risk. And it's almost impossible to assess risk without having this data, so the EPA has pretty much given up on trying to force testing. Yes, you read that right—*almost all the chemicals in your home today have undergone no meaningful testing of any kind.*

The Consumer Product Safety Commission requires that cleaning product labels warn people of immediate dangers, as well as any toxic ingredients. These warnings are given by signal words on labels such as "Danger" or "Warning." Unfortunately, there are a lot of loopholes to this law. Manufacturers don't need to state what *kind* of danger a substance poses—only what not to do, such as "do not take internally." And they don't need to list a warning of a substance at all if they have determined (by their own research) that exposure would not trigger a toxic effect. And if there is no data one way or another on whether a particular substance is toxic (which is, remember, the case for thousands of chemicals in use), then they don't have to give any warning either.

A study by the Environmental Working Group tested the umbilical-cord blood of 10 American babies born in 2004 and found an average of 200 industrial chemicals and pollutants in each baby's blood.

products were harmful you would have heard about them by now. People would be suing the companies that make cleaning products that damaged their health. Congress would have passed laws against them. You'd be sick yourself if they were so bad, right? The problem is the *amount* of harmful ingredients in any given cleaning product. It is tiny, so ill effects don't usually appear immediately.

But here's the kicker: the effects are *cumulative*. Toxins build up in your body over time. This is what scientists are now calling "body burden." Americans, today, have hundreds of synthetic chemicals running through our bodies.

They are stored in our cells. In fact, now our babies are born with these chemicals in their systems, passed from mother to child in the womb. The EPA estimates that every American has more than 700 pollutants in his or her body. And we have no way of knowing how this kind of chronic, low-dose exposure will affect people over the course of their lives.

Deciding What's Safe

Most products undergo some testing before they are put on the shelves and sold to consumers. It's mainly done out of sheer self-preservation—companies don't want to deal with costly lawsuits if their product ends up being harmful.

The problem is, these products are tested individually. Testing attempts to determine whether regular use of one particular product causes any ill effects. But no one uses just one product. You probably have dozens in your home right now. So if you combine two or more products that each contain the same "safe level" of one particular ingredient, you will create a mixture that now has an unsafe level of that ingredient.

On top of that, chemicals from different products mix together in unpredictable ways. They may mix in your body—or in a stream—and create something much more toxic. For instance, scientists have found that, in some cases, triclosan, a common antibacterial additive to everything from hand soaps to countertops, can be converted by sunlight into a type of dioxin—one of the deadliest pollutants ever made. The sum can indeed be greater (or more harmful) than its parts.

How They Get In

You may think that as long as you're not foolish enough to eat or drink a cleaning product it's not getting into your body. Unfortunately, you can absorb chemicals in all sorts of ways. First, of course, is your skin. Any time you touch a cleaning solution, a small amount is absorbed by your skin and enters your bloodstream. Spray cleaners are particularly problematic—even if you wear gloves, sprays suspend particles of cleaning solution in the air, where they can settle on any unprotected area, such as your face and arms.

Green Fact

According to the American Cancer Society, the probability that a resident of the United States will develop cancer at some point in his or her lifetime is 1 in 2 for men and 1 in 3 for women. Approximately 1,450,000 new cancer cases were expected to be diagnosed in 2007.

Many of our nation's youth are afflicted with asthma, and it's a good bet that cleaning products are one culprit.

And many cleaning products don't rinse away completely. They leave a residue that can be picked up on the skin of any family member merely by touching a surface that has been cleaned. This happens to my son with detergent residue all the time when he's visiting other people's homes. And this residue can turn into a dust that gets into the air and circulates throughout your home. Which brings me to your lungs. You breathe chemicals into your lungs when you spray while cleaning. And even if you're not spraying a product, most cleaning products contain volatile organic compounds (VOCs). These chemical compounds give off gases that are easily absorbed by your lungs. From your lungs they enter your bloodstream. These particles and gases can stay suspended in the air for a long period of time, so even if you wait to clean until your kids are at school, they can still inhale this stuff when they get home. So, to put a new twist on the phrase "you are what you eat," you are what you breathe. For a rundown of the diseases that are associated with the toxic ingredients found in many cleaners. (See the Appendix on page 212.)

WHY KIDS ARE MORE VULNERABLE

Children are much more sensitive than adults to chemicals in the environment. Exposure to a chemical that causes no discernible effect in an adult can cause significant harm to an infant. Some reasons for this include:

❑ Children frequently have their hands in their mouths, making it more likely that they will ingest toxins with which they come in contact.

❑ Children have a faster metabolism—pound for pound, children eat more food and breathe more air than adults.

❑ Children play on the floor, where many toxins in the home settle.

❑ Children's metabolic pathways are immature, and they are less able to detoxify and excrete toxins that get into their system.

❑ Children are undergoing rapid development, and organ systems that are disrupted while in the middle of growing may fail to form correctly.

❑ Children have more years for toxins to accumulate in their bodies and reach unsafe levels.

"Children are really the heart of the green-clean movement. When we talk about clean air and clean water, it really comes down to what is best for our kids." – J.S.

THE ENVIRONMENTAL IMPACT

The thousands of product choices on our grocery-store shelves put a heavy burden on our environment.

Depletion of Nonrenewable Resources

Fuel is used to farm crops, run mining equipment, refine raw materials, power factories, and ship products to stores. Crude oil is converted into hundreds of different chemicals, as well as the plastics used to package those chemicals. Water, while technically a renewable resource, is used at a faster rate than it is replenished in many areas. It is estimated that the vast Ogallala Aquifer in the American Midwest, which runs from North Dakota to Texas, will be pumped dry within decades if current irrigation practices aren't drastically changed.

Air Pollution

Global warming has gotten a lot of attention in recent years, for good reasons. Cleaning products certainly produce their fair share of greenhouse gases during their production.

Habitat Destruction

Raw materials for cleaning products—minerals, plants, and crude oil—need to be extracted from the earth. Land is cleared for crops, earth is mined for minerals, and oil wells and pipelines are constructed, all of which disrupt native animal, bird, and plant species. The debate over drilling oil in Alaska's Arctic Wildlife Refuge illustrates how the extraction of raw materials can be detrimental.

Petroleum-based products are particularly energy-intensive. Turning black crude oil into a pretty pink dish soap is a complex process. In addition to greenhouse gases, many other toxins can be released into the air. For instance, one method of creating chlorine can discharge mercury into the air.

Cleaning products are often sources of water pollution.

And let's not forget indoor air pollution. The air in today's homes is more polluted than outdoors—even in cities that are notoriously polluted. Cleaning products play a significant role in indoor air pollution because many of them contain ingredients that are VOCs. These compounds are "volatile" because they easily become vapors or gases. These vapors and gases leave your cleaning solution and drift into the air, where they can be absorbed into your lungs.

Water Pollution

Both mining and farm operations, which deal with raw materials, can pollute waterways in the name of cleaning. For example, crops such as corn and soy beans—ironically often the main ingredients in vegetable-based cleaning products—are grown with pesticides and herbicides. Eventually, these chemicals, however minute in quantity, find their way back into the water.

Oil refineries and other manufacturing plants, all part of the cleaning industry, produce a lot of waste. And sometimes they are allowed to dump it into lakes and rivers. For instance, in August 2007 the BP oil refinery in Whiting, Indiana, was in the news because it was issued a new permit to release significantly more ammonia and "suspended solids" into Lake

Even small contributions to the green movement can help keep our water sparkling.

Cleaning products we use at home make their way into our water systems.

FINDING QUALITY ECO-PRODUCTS

If you wish to buy ready-made environmentally friendly products, your best bet is a health-food store. There are plenty of independent stores out there, and Wild Oats, Trader Joe's, and Whole Foods are three national chains that specialize in eco-friendly products.

It's often better to evaluate a company rather than one specific product. Do some research on the company and take a look at its Web site and its packaging. Some companies are guilty of what's called "green washing"—they have an eco-sounding name and packaging and say they are nontoxic, but when it comes right down to it they differ little from their conventional counterparts. Anyone can use words such as "nontoxic," "all-natural," and "environmentally friendly" because there are no regulations preventing it.

Look for companies that follow most of these policies:

❏ They reveal all ingredients on their labels and the ingredient names are specific, not vague.

❏ Their products are "readily biodegradable" within days (not years).

❏ Their products contain plant-based ingredients, not petroleum-based ones.

❏ They use natural essential oils instead of artificial fragrances—or their products are fragrance-free.

Read labels at the store and avoid the following:

❏ Any product with the words "Poison," "Warning," or "Danger" on the label (The word "Caution" is okay.)

❏ Ingredients with chemical names that include "chlor," "phenol," "glycol," or end in "-ene"

❏ Any product that is "combustible" or "flammable"

❏ Any product that should be used in a well-ventilated room

Michigan. (See the Appendix on page 212 for the dangers of ammonia.)

When cleaning products are used at home in sinks, toilets, showers, dishwashers, and washing machines, they make their way into lakes, streams, and rivers through septic systems and waste-water treatment plants.

The old saying "what goes around comes around" is certainly true when it comes to the chemicals that get into our water. They almost always make their way back into our bodies. Even if the drinking water in your area isn't contaminated, chemicals may get into the irrigation systems used for crops or to feed livestock—so it comes back around to you in your food.

For further reading on cleaning chemicals and their health and environmental impacts, I recommend "Naturally Clean: The Seventh Generation Guide to Safe & Healthy, Non-Toxic Cleaning" by Jeffrey Hollender.

According to the American Lung Association, the Environmental Protection Agency (EPA) ranks poor indoor air quality among the top five risks to public health. The EPA reports that levels of air pollution inside the home can be two to five times higher than outdoor levels.

WHAT YOU CAN DO

So how do you protect yourself, your loved ones, and the earth from the thousands of chemicals that are out there? Well, greening up your cleaning is a great place to start. By sticking to ingredients that have been used for hundreds of years with no known toxic effects, and purchasing products from reputable companies that have demonstrated a significant commitment to the environment, you can greatly reduce the harmful chemicals in your life.

Humans have been cleaning their homes since we first established permanent settlements almost 10,000 years ago. Most chemicals in use today have been created in the last 75 years. It helps to remember this when you think about giving up conventional cleaners. They aren't necessary. The best and safest cleaning products are those that have been around forever. You probably have them in your kitchen already: baking soda, vinegar, borax, washing soda, oxygen bleach, lemon juice, liquid soap, and club soda. Check out Chapter 2 to find out all about these basics ingredients and how to combine them in simple recipes to clean just about every surface of your home.

I've covered many compelling reasons to switch to green cleaning in this chapter. An added benefit is that it can save you money. If you make at least a few of your own cleaners at home from my recipes, you will be amazed at just how cheap cleaning can be. Most of the ingredients can be purchased in bulk. Baking soda, for example, is available in 12-pound bags. If you're truly on a budget, you won't need anything besides a liquid soap, baking soda, and vinegar—those three products can clean your whole house!

No time to make your own? Ready-made green cleaners are available at health-food stores and supermarkets.

Your New Cleaning Arsenal

When I first changed my cleaning methods, I just started buying nontoxic brands at my local health-food store. It simply made sense to me because it's always better to be safe than sorry. But my son's allergy to detergents forced me to really get "back to basics." And basics is what this chapter is all about.

I was amazed at how well these simple ingredients work. I found myself regaling my friends with stories of my latest baking-soda cleaning triumph. And when I discovered essential oils, I really started to enjoy things. It's like aromatherapy every time I clean. Don't get me wrong—cleaning is still something I'd rather avoid—but using homemade cleaners is as good as it gets.

Green-cleaning supplies are surprisingly simple and inexpensive. Versatile products, such as baking soda, left, can be used for everything from cleaning your oven to brushing your teeth.

"Toss out the chemicals and load up on vinegar, baking soda, lemons, and soap."

Every green cleaner should have the following at home:

Liquid Soap

A mild liquid soap can be used to clean almost anything, and it is an ingredient in most of the recipes I've listed at the end of this chapter. I recommend a true soap product, such as Dr. Bronner's Castile Soap. A plant-based hand-dishwashing detergent from a reputable nontoxic brand, such as Seventh Generation, would be my second choice. (For more on detergents versus soaps, see page 18.)

Liquid soap may seem expensive at first, but it is concentrated and a little goes a long way. A gallon seems to last forever.

Borax (Sodium Borate)

Borax is a mineral similar in properties to baking soda, but it has a higher pH and is therefore stronger. Like baking soda, it can remove odor, soften water, and dissolve dirt. In addition, it has antifungal and antibacterial properties and can kill mold and mildew. Although natural, borax is toxic when ingested, so be sure to keep it out of the reach of children. You can find it in the laundry-detergent section at the grocery store. The most common brand is 20 Mule Team Borax by Dial.

Baking Soda (Sodium Bicarbonate)

Baking soda is a naturally occurring mineral. I rely more on it than any other single cleaning ingredient. It removes odor, softens water, dissolves dirt and grime, scrubs soap scum, unclogs drains, cleans ovens, and more. It truly is the first "miracle" cleaning product. In fact, using baking-soda paste on my glass shower doors convinced me that I no longer needed any conventional cleaning products.

Washing Soda (Sodium Carbonate)

This mineral is highest on the pH scale and therefore has the most cleaning power and is also the most caustic. It is an effective abrasive cleanser and can boost the power of laundry detergents. Avoid using it on fiberglass, aluminum,

Phosphates are banned from most cleaning products, but automatic dishwashing detergents have an exemption and can still contain up to 20 percent phosphates. Phosphates that end up in our waterways cause algae blooms that deplete oxygen and kill off fish.

no-wax floors, and delicate fabrics. It can irritate the skin, so use gloves when cleaning with it. Like Borax, washing soda can also be found in the laundry section. Arm & Hammer Super Washing Soda is a popular brand.

White Distilled Vinegar

Vinegar is a mild acid that readily dissolves soap scum, cleans glass, disinfects surfaces, and is a perfect natural fabric softener. Always use distilled white vinegar because apple cider or wine vinegar can stain.

Lemon Juice

Another mild acid, lemon juice also has mild bleaching properties. It is a great stain remover and whitener. Fresh-squeezed lemon juice is best, but bottled lemon juice can be used in a pinch.

Oxygen Bleach

Powdered oxygen bleach is a great alternative to chlorine bleach and is friendlier to you and the environment because it is usually sodium percarbonate (a mixture of hydrogen peroxide and washing soda). It is especially useful for whitening laundry, removing stains from fabric, and cleaning grout. For maximum cleaning power, look for a content of 75 percent sodium percarbonate. And avoid those that have added artificial fragrance or dye.

SAFETY RULES

Even natural ingredients can be toxic if ingested, and some can be irritating to skin and eyes. Take the following precautions, especially if you have children in your home.

❏ Label the cleaner containers clearly, and store them out of the reach of children.

❏ Always tape the recipe for a homemade cleaner to its container. This is important in case a child ingests some and you (or a babysitter) need to tell the poison control center exactly what was in it.

❏ Only follow recipes from reputable sources. Remember that "homemade" doesn't always mean "nontoxic." Many highly questionable recipes can be found on the Internet.

❏ Be aware that some chemical combinations are hazardous—the classic example is bleach and ammonia.

❏ If you have small children, consider leaving essential oils out of homemade cleaners because the nice smells may entice children to taste. (My son dove into my lemon-scented dishwasher soap!)

Essential oils come in small bottles, but you use just a few drops at a time so the bottles last a long time.

Club Soda

This beverage contains the mineral sodium citrate, which helps it loosen dirt and soften water so that it dries without water spots. It is great for cleaning glass and appliances and removing stains from fabrics. Avoid types marked "low sodium" because they may have a lower mineral content, which would make them less effective.

Aloe extract is commonly used in eco-friendly dishwashing liquids for its healing properties.

Essential Oils

Essential oils make cleaning with homemade cleaners a lot more enjoyable. Common ones include lavender, lemon, orange, peppermint, and tea tree. Essential oils can also be used for their disinfectant properties. Lavender and tea tree oils, in particular, have been shown to have antibacterial and antifungal properties. You can find essential oils at your local health-food store, or order them online. Look for ones that say "100 percent pure" to avoid unwanted additives. If you are using oils for disinfecting purposes, spend a little more and get high-quality organic ones. Use metal spoons, not plastic ones, when measuring them.

Acid Versus Basic

When choosing an ingredient for cleaning, it's important to know whether you need an acid (low pH) or base (high pH).

ACID CLEANERS	USE ON ANY
Lemon juice	Rust
Olive oil	Soap scum
Club soda	Water spots
Vinegar	

BASIC CLEANERS	USE ON ANY
Soap	Body oil
Baking soda	Food stains
Borax	General dirt and grime
Washing soda	

All-Surface Spray

This spray is effective on everyday dirt and grime, wipes up without leaving any residue, and is safe to use on most surfaces. Use it to clean counters, walls, spills, and more. Note that in many situations, warm water and a microfiber cloth is all you really need. But when you need to add a little more "oomph" to your cleaning, try the following recipe:

1 16-oz. spray bottle
2 tsps. borax
hot water
1/4 tsp. liquid castile soap

Using Store-Bought?

Avoid spray cleaners containing ammonia, bleach, alcohol, butyl cellosolve, petroleum-based detergents, dyes, and fragrances.

Put the borax in the spray bottle, fill the bottle with hot water, shake until the borax is dissolved, and then add the soap. Spray on surfaces, let it sit a minute or two, and wipe off with a sponge or microfiber cloth.

All-Purpose Liquid Cleaner

This formula is ideal for washing floors, cars, and any other large jobs for which you would want to make a large batch in a bucket.

1 gal. hot water
1 tbsp. baking soda
2 tbsps. liquid soap
   or detergent

Fill a bucket with hot water, and then add baking soda and soap. (Adding soap last prevents it from foaming too much.) Add 1 tablespoon of washing soda if you've got heavy grease to remove, or 1 tablespoon of borax if you also want to disinfect or kill mildew.

Using Store-Bought?
Avoid commercial liquid cleaners containing ammonia, bleach, alcohol, butyl cellosolve, petroleum-based detergents, dyes, and artificial fragrances.

"Microfiber cloths are made from petroleum-based fabrics, but I feel that their longevity, combined with their chemical-free cleaning power, make them worthwhile." – J. S.

Glass Cleaner

Spray cleaners fill the air with a fine mist that you can't help inhaling. Many of the commercial ingredients are irritating to the lungs. Also, conventional glass cleaners often include petroleum-based waxes, which leave a film on the glass.

1 cup distilled white vinegar

1 cup water

$\frac{1}{2}$ tsp. liquid dish soap (optional)

3–8 drops essential oil (optional)

Fill the spray bottle with vinegar and water, and shake gently. If you don't like the smell of vinegar, add essential oil. Soap is needed to dissolve the waxy buildup left behind by conventional cleaners—once the buildup is gone you can leave out the soap. For more information on cleaning windows, see page 108.

Using Store-Bought?

Avoid cleaners containing ammonia, butyl cellosolve, naphtha, glycol ethers, wax, phosphoric acid, methanol, isopropyl alcohol, dioxane, petroleum-based detergents, formaldehyde, dyes, and fragrance.

Dishwasher Powder

This recipe works wonderfully for me, although you may need to prerinse your dishes because it's not quite as effective on baked-on food. Citric acid (also called sour salt) is the key ingredient, and you can buy it in bulk online. (See Resources.) You may be able to find it at places that sell canning supplies. This recipe also makes a great scouring powder.

¼ cup citric acid

1½ cups borax

15 drops essential oil (optional)

Put all ingredients in a plastic container with a tight-fitting lid and shake well. Use about 1 tablespoon per load. Shake each time before using. If you have particularly hard water, increase the amount you use with each load.

Using Store-Bought?

The hot temperatures of dishwashers vaporize toxins in detergents and release them into your kitchen. Chlorine, phosphates, and antibacterials are ingredients to avoid.

Laundry Soap

Making your own laundry soap is a great way to keep your family's clothing chemical free.

⅛ cup liquid soap or detergent
1 tbsp. washing soda
¼ cup vinegar

Add the liquid soap and washing soda to the washing machine as it fills with water. Try varying the amount of ingredients to fine-tune the recipe for your needs. If you're using soap (not detergent), use a warm-water wash. Increase the amount of washing soda if your water is very hard. Add the vinegar to the rinse cycle (not the wash cycle!) to rinse away soap scum and soften clothes. Vinegar alleviates the need to use any fabric softener at all. For particularly dirty loads, or to whiten whites, use oxygen (non-chlorine) bleach. For more details, see the chapter on laundry starting on page 92.

Using Store-Bought?

Avoid conventional fabric softeners, chlorine bleach, and Fels Naptha soap. Fabric softeners in particular have nasty chemicals that coat your clothes and directly contact your skin.

Mildew and Germ Killer

Use this spray in the kitchen and bathroom—anywhere that you want to kill germs. Preliminary research shows that it has broad antibacterial, antifungal, and antiviral properties. Studies have shown that lavender oil is antibacterial as well. Essential oils can be found at most health- food stores or ordered online.

1 16-oz. spray bottle
2 cups water
¼ tsp. (about 25 drops) tea tree oil
¼ tsp. (about 25 drops) lavender oil

Note that we cannot officially call this a "disinfectant" because it has not been classified as such by the FDA. Fill the spray bottle with water, and then add the tea tree and lavender oils. Shake gently before each use.
Spray on surfaces, and leave to dry—do not wipe.
(See "Mold and Mildew" on page 62.)

Using Store-Bought?

Avoid disinfectants containing cresol, phenol, ethanol, kerosene, formaldehyde, ammonia, chlorine bleach, sodium hydroxide, and phosphoric acid.

Baking Soda Scrub

This is a great all-purpose mild cleanser that scrubs and lifts dirt at the same time. It's effective for cleaning grout, stovetops, sinks, and just about anything else.

2 tbsps. baking soda
liquid dish soap or castile soap

Put baking soda in a widemouthed container and mix in the liquid soap a little bit at a time until you have a nice foamy paste. Work onto the surface you wish to clean using a rag, sponge, or brush (depending on how much abrasion you need). Let it sit 1 to 15 minutes (longer for heavy-duty jobs, shorter for light cleaning), and then spray with vinegar to rinse. If you are working with a surface that is sensitive to acids (such as tile), rinse off the vinegar immediately with water.

Using Store-Bought?

Avoid chlorine bleach, a common additive to powdered cleansers and soft scrubs. It irritates the lungs, skin, and eyes and is a major cause of poisoning in children under age 6.

WHERE TO START

Sometimes it's overwhelming to think about changing all the products and methods you use to clean your home. Here are some tips to help you get started.

1. Throw Out

Here's a quick list of the most toxic products in your home that you should dispose of immediately. Take them to the nearest household hazardous-waste collection site. You can find safe alternatives for all of these items in this book.

- ❑ Drain cleaners
- ❑ Oven cleaners
- ❑ Toilet bowl cleaners
- ❑ Fabric softeners
- ❑ Furniture polishes
- ❑ Air fresheners
- ❑ Chlorine bleach
- ❑ Ammonia

Most cleaning recipes require little more than products you probably already have on your shelves.

Tools for mixing your homemade recipes include measuring cups and widemouthed containers.

2. Stock Up

Head to the grocery store and stock up on the following products:

- ❑ Baking soda
- ❑ Borax
- ❑ White vinegar
- ❑ Club soda
- ❑ Oxygen bleach

3. Gear Up

Even if you don't want to make many homemade cleaners, these tools are a must:

- ❑ Spray bottles
- ❑ Widemouthed containers with tight lids
- ❑ Measuring cups and spoons
- ❑ Microfiber cloths
- ❑ Cotton rags
- ❑ Cellulose sponges
- ❑ Dust mop
- ❑ Broom
- ❑ Dust pan
- ❑ Bucket

An important aspect of green cleaning is avoiding one-use, throwaway materials. Select quality cleaning tools that you can use more than once.

Microfiber cloths: These cloths can be found just about everywhere these days, and they are well worth buying. The unique weave of the cloth allows it to pick up dirt and grime with ease. Much of your everyday cleaning chores can be done with just a microfiber cloth and water. Special cloths formulated for glass can even be used without water. Just throw them in the washing machine when they get dirty.

Cloth rags: Cotton rags are useful for almost any cleaning project. Use them in place of sponges—they last longer

Only When Needed

Disinfectants are hugely overused in the United States. There are only three home cleaning situations where I believe that more than soap and water is warranted: 1) if you have an immune-compromised person in your home; 2) in the kitchen to protect against food-borne bacteria; and 3) to kill mold and mildew.

As an alternative to the Mildew and Germ Killer recipe on page 43, use white vinegar. It is perfect for everyday cleaning where you would like to disinfect a bit, too. Studies referenced by Heinz show that it kills 99 percent of bacteria, 82 percent of mold, and 80 percent of germs (viruses).

and can be thrown in the washing machine so that they don't lie around gathering bacteria. If your family doesn't provide you with enough old clothes for rags, buy some. A kind of cloth diaper called "Chinese Prefolds" makes a great absorbent rag that is perfect for cleaning spills.

Brushes: A large wooden brush with soft, natural bristles is great for large cleaning projects. Toothbrushes are great for getting into nooks and crannies. (I recommend using a new toothbrush because the bristles of used ones are too soft to be effective.)

Bucket: Buy a high-quality plastic or stainless-steel bucket that will stand up to abuse and last for years.

Squeegee: A squeegee is great for washing windows and mirrors and shower walls and doors. It saves you

Natural Sponges

Choose sponges made of cellulose that are not treated with antibacterials. (They typically say something like "resists odors.") Or opt for an even more natural sea sponge. Loofahs work great for abrasive scrubbing. Boil your sponge or throw it in the microwave (2 minutes) to disinfect it.

from having to wipe down glass with a rag or paper towel.

Timer: Often, a nontoxic cleaner works better if it's allowed to sit for several minutes. An inexpensive kitchen timer will allow you to walk away and do another quick chore without forgetting to come back and finish the job.

Caddy: A plastic caddy is a convenient way to store essential cleaning products and carry them around.

Broom: Reach for your broom instead of the vacuum to do a quick cleanup—you'll save energy and burn calories. Angled nylon brooms pick up dirt well, although corn brooms are a more eco-friendly option.

Dust pan and brush: If you're going to use a broom, you've got to have a dust pan. Look for one that is wide and

A caddy makes it easy to transfer your cleaning supplies from one job site to the next.

sturdy, preferably made of metal.

Dust mop: A dust mop is great for quick floor cleanups. It picks up finer particles than brooms and doesn't use electricity like a vacuum. It is also great for lifting cobwebs off walls and ceilings. Look for one that has a removable pad that can be machine washed.

Mop: There are many different types of mops. I prefer microfiber ones, but string and sponge mops work well, too.

Be sure that you rinse them well and let them dry out thoroughly between cleanings; otherwise they will attract mold. (For more information on mops and other floor tools, see Chapter 7.)

Vacuums: See "Buying a Vacuum" on page 50.

Steam cleaners: See the following page for how these units are used and for tips on buying.

The long hose on this canister-style vacuum allows it to be used for off-the-floor chores, such as dusting and cleaning blinds. The power nozzle, shown, does an excellent job on carpets.

STEAM CLEANING

A steam cleaner is a truly ideal green product. It cleans and disinfects with minimal effort and no chemicals. The only drawbacks are that it uses quite a bit of energy (about the same as a vacuum), and the high-quality ones are expensive (about $500 to $2,000). But if you have allergies or multiple-chemical sensitivity, you should consider one. A steam cleaner works great on showers, ovens, upholstery, countertops, and bare floors—and it kills bacteria, mold, and dust mites.

Look for a "vapor" steam cleaner that produces "dry steam." Ones that have a boiler temperature of at least 245 degrees and a warranty on the boiler of at least 3 years are best. Make sure you choose one that will run at least an hour before it needs refilling.

Steam cleaners usually come with multiple attachments for cleaning different surfaces.

They can be used in place of a mop to clean and disinfect any type of bare flooring from tile to wood.

Small brush attachments allow you to remove mold and soap scum from tile with ease. They're also great for stubborn stains, such as grout between tile.

BUYING A VACUUM

From a green-cleaning perspective, the best vacuums are the ones that completely trap dust and dirt (and the allergens and chemical residues they contain) and prevent them from escaping back into your home. If you have allergies or multiple-chemical sensitivity, my recommendation is to buy the best vacuum you can afford. When researching vacuums, consider the following:

Canister or Upright: If you have mostly carpeting and rugs, an upright is your best choice because it is usually more powerful and has a beater bar that agitates the carpet fibers and shakes the dirt loose. A canister is lighter and more maneuverable and is well suited to bare floors. Its long hose allows you to clean curtains, furniture, and stairs with ease.

An unpowered brush attachment is the preferred tool for hardwood floors.

An upholstery attachment concentrates the suction so it can pull dust from textured fabrics.

Beater Bars: If you have a mix of carpeting and bare floors, look for an upright that can be used on bare floors (usually by turning off the beater bar). Or buy a canister that comes with a "power head" motorized attachment for carpets.

Tools: If you plan on using attachments frequently, look for a model that allows you to store tools right on the vacuum.

Bags and Filters: Consider the environmental impact of disposing of vacuum bags and filters. Be sure to ask what needs to be replaced before you buy. Bagless vacuums seem to be more eco friendly, as long as they don't require frequent filter changes.

If you have a bag vacuum, be sure to empty the bag when it gets half full—after that it starts to lose sucking power and you waste energy.

HEPA Filtration: The standard for allergy sufferers is HEPA filtration. However, not all HEPA vacuums are equal. Consumer Reports found that the level of dust emissions depended as much on the vacuum design as it did the type of filtration. Look for models with a "completely sealed" HEPA system.

Durability: The longer your vacuum lasts, the fewer you'll end up sending to the landfill. Look for a company with a reputation for durability that offers a long warranty (5 years or more) on its products. Consider buying a commercial vacuum if you can afford one.

Vacuums with porous filters pick up small particles and then reintroduce them to the home. This bagless vacuum cleaner includes a high-performance filtering system, which prevents that.

INSIDE JOBS Part II

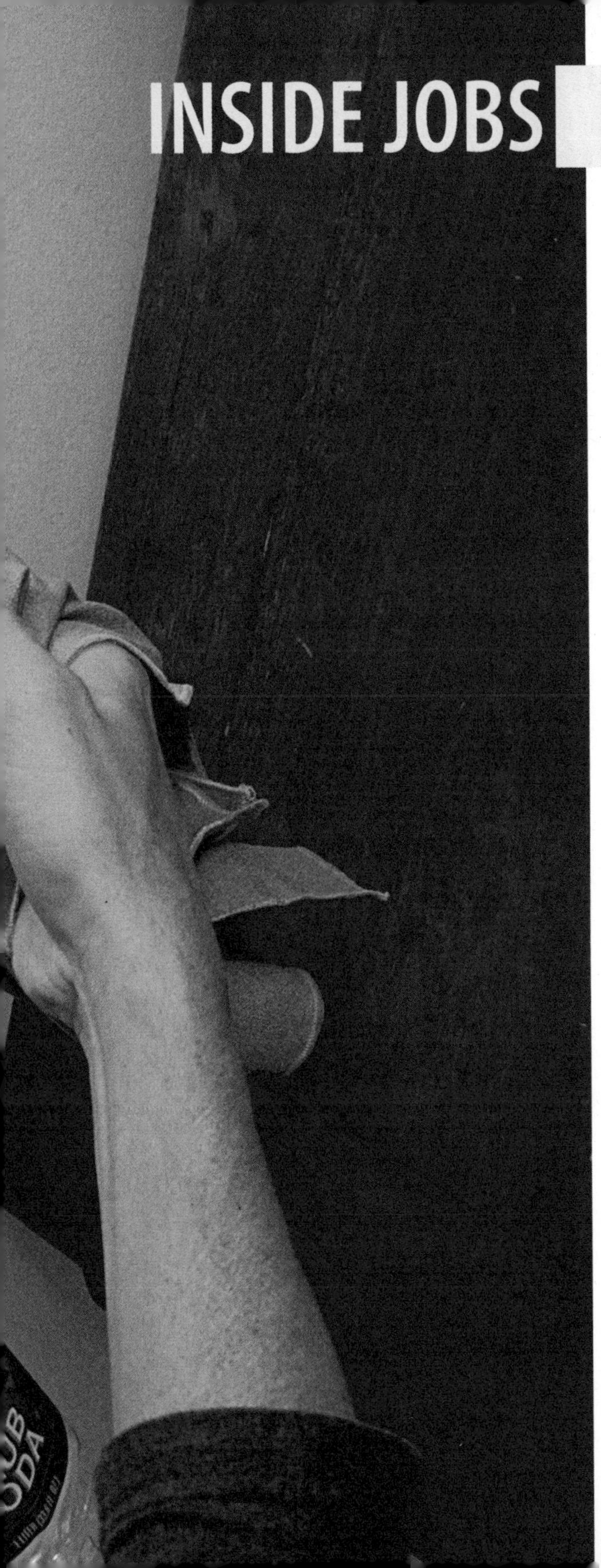

The Fresh Bathroom

How many times have you used a cleaning product in the bathroom and had your eyes water and your nose burn from the fumes? This discomfort isn't merely an inconvenience. It's evidence that you are being exposed to toxins. It's your body's way of telling you to "get away quickly." But you ignore what your body is trying to tell you because your bathroom has to be clean, right?

For me, the bathroom was one of the hardest areas to "go green." Bathrooms are full of germs, and you need a powerful disinfectant, right? Turns out both assumptions are wrong: kitchens have more germs than bathrooms (by far), and plain soap and vinegar do a fine job of germ killing without harsh chemicals.

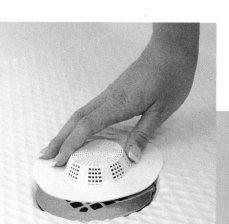

Prevention is one of the keys to avoiding toxic chemicals. Using a hair catcher, left, stops clogs in shower drains before they start. Simple cleaning methods eliminate toxins from your home.

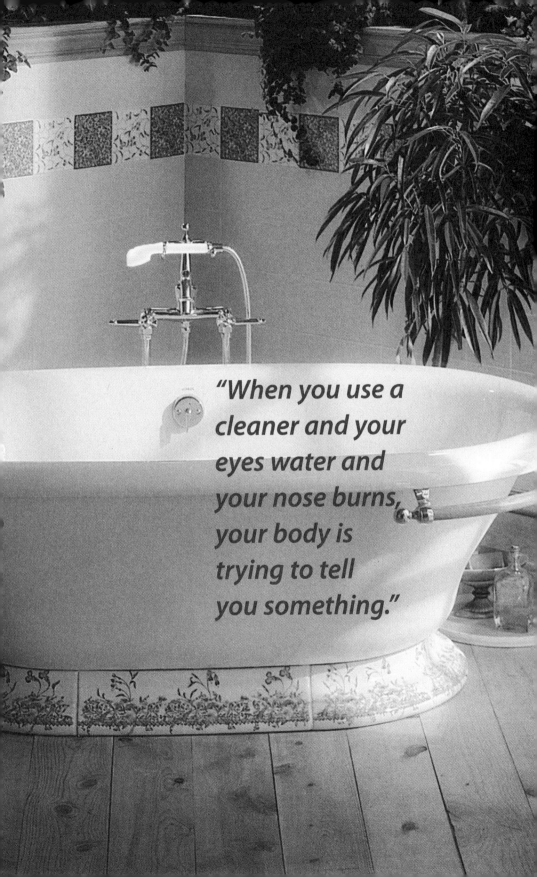

"When you use a cleaner and your eyes water and your nose burns, your body is trying to tell you something."

While waterproof and durable, most shower and tub materials are—somewhat paradoxically—vulnerable to scratching. Acrylic and fiberglass are probably the most notorious to easily scratch. Porcelain (also called enameled steel or enameled cast iron) looks tough, but it is actually a glass surface fused to a metal base. Vitreous china and glazed ceramic tile have a similar finish, and for this reason, they can be scratched. Even manufacturers of solid-surfacing material recommend avoiding abrasives. So where does that leave you? Well, it means you'll need to rely instead on nonabrasive cleaners—and plenty of elbow grease.

The one exception to this is if the surface has already been scratched. In that case, you may need to use an abrasive cleaner or scrub brush to get grime out of the scratches. As you can imagine, this is a downward spiral, with the scratching getting worse and the sur-

Soap Scum

Soap scum occurs when soap combines with minerals that are in the water. Essentially the soap encapsulates the dirt and oil with which it comes into contact, and minerals, such as calcium, make it insoluble. That's why soap scum sticks to the side of your tub. The film builds up and everything starts to look grimy. The harder the water, the more minerals it contains, which worsens the problem. Use one of the methods on pages 57 or 58 to keep buildup to a minimum. (Note: these recommendations are based on semi-hard water. If you have very hard or very soft water you will need to adjust the methods accordingly, at least for your initial cleaning.)

face getting harder and harder to clean. In this situation, you will definitely want to adopt the preventative measure of wiping your bath down to dry it off after each use. (See the opposite page.) Some types of surfaces can be refinished, including solid-surfacing materials, so you may want to explore that option as well.

[smart tip]

Tile and Acid Don't Mix

Don't use vinegar or other acids on tile on a frequent basis. Both the tile and the grout can be etched by the acid. Test in an inconspicuous spot first, and wait 24 hours to see if any discoloration occurs, especially if you have colored grout.

Shower Doors

Glass shower doors are a challenge to keep sparkling. In a moment of temporary insanity, my husband and I bought clear glass ones for our shower. I use a combination of methods to keep them clean. I squeegee the doors after each use, and scrub them with the **Baking-Soda Scrub on page 44** whenever they start to look dingy. The paste works amazingly well—better than any commercial cleaner I've ever used. Don't forget to clean the shower door tracks: plug the drain holes with a bit of paper towel; fill the tracks with vinegar; and let it sit overnight. Then rinse and wipe dry.

Preventing Soap Scum and Mold

What you'll need: squeegee, sponge, or towel

Using a squeegee, large sponge, or absorbent towel, take a minute to remove the beads of water from the walls, floor, and ceiling of your tub or shower after each use. This helps remove soap and mineral deposits before they harden, and it also removes the moisture that mold and mildew need to thrive. If you use a sponge or towel, be sure to allow it to dry completely between uses—alternating two is a good idea.

Squeegeeing your shower after each use is an easy way to keep it clean and avoid scrubbing.

*Use your nose—as soon as sponges or towels smell musty, launder the towel or disinfect the sponge in the microwave. (See page 79.) If you can get all family members to adopt this habit, you probably won't have to really "clean" your shower. Just shine things up using the **Glass Cleaner recipe on page 40** or your favorite nontoxic product.*

Removing Mild Buildup

What you'll need: white vinegar, a spray bottle, and a nonabrasive sponge

Spray the surface heavily with undiluted vinegar, let it sit for 10 minutes (not less), and then scrub it using a nonabrasive sponge. This works best if you microwave the vinegar first so that it is fairly hot (but not burning). Repeat if needed.

Plain vinegar is often enough to remove light soap scum. The key is to really saturate the area.

Removing Moderate Buildup

What you'll need: baking soda, water, and a nonabrasive sponge

Prepare a paste by putting a cup of baking soda in a widemouthed container and slowly adding water until it thickens. Rub in the paste with your fingers or a nonabrasive sponge. Then rinse it off with vinegar and plenty of water.

A microfiber sponge is effective for nonabrasive scrubbing.

"My bathroom is challenging with clear shower doors and white tile floors, but I manage to keep them sparkling with just soap, vinegar, and baking soda." – J.S.

Hard water is one cause of clogged showerheads. If you've got irregular streams of water, try this: fill a plastic sandwich bag with vinegar and tie it around the showerhead using a wire tie or rubber band. Allow the showerhead to soak for several hours or overnight. Then remove the bag and scrub the showerhead using a brush.

WATER CONSERVATION

From showers and toilets to sinks and dishwashers, water flows out of your home at an alarming rate. Using eco-friendly cleaners helps lessen your waste water's impact on the environment, but using less water overall is equally important.

❏ When hand-washing dishes, try not to rinse them under running water. If you have a double-bowl sink, use one bowl for washing and fill the other with hot water for rinsing. If not, use a plastic basin for rinsing.

❏ Only run the dishwasher or washing machine when it is full. It takes less water to run one full load than two partial loads.

❏ Fix leaks as soon as you notice them. Not only do they waste water, but they become a breeding ground for mold, mildew, and insects. Fix that toilet that doesn't stop running, too.

❏ Use the minimum amount of soap or detergent necessary for a cleaning job. Too much soap means you'll have to waste water rinsing it off of whatever you're cleaning.

❏ Read the instruction manuals for your dishwasher and washing machine to find out the cycles that are shortest and use the least amount of water. You may find you can get away with a shorter cycle—and if you use cold water you can reduce your energy use, too.

❏ When purchasing dishwashers, washing machines, and water heaters look for ones with a high Energy Star rating. Consider a high-efficiency front-loading washing machine. (See page 95 for more information on selecting a washing machine.)

When designing a new bathroom, keep fixtures off the floor to make cleaning easy.

Mold and mildew are particularly tough cleaning foes. There's nothing yuckier than black and green spots crawling along your grout lines and up your shower curtain—not to mention mold's toxic affects on air quality. Mold spores have been linked to rashes, congestion, fatigue, headaches, chronic sinusitis, as well as other afflictions in more in sensitive individuals. You may be used to turning to bleach immediately when you see mold rear its ugly head, but there are ways to fight it that don't involve harming your lungs and skin. (For more on the dangers of chlorine, see the Appendix.)

Stop It Before It Starts

Preventing mold from growing in the first place is obviously the ideal non-toxic solution. What prevention really comes down to is humidity. Take away moisture and mold can't grow. Here are some tips to help you make your bathroom as dry as possible:

· **A bathroom venting fan** is your first line of defense. Make sure it is rated to fit the size of your bathroom. One rule of thumb: a fan must exhaust 1 cubic foot per minute (CFM) for every square foot. So, a 40-square-foot bathroom needs a fan rated for 40 CFM. Run the fan during your shower and afterward for at least 20 minutes. Replace your standard wall switch with a wall-switch timer. (See page 69.)

· **Keep a thermometer** that also measures humidity or a hygrometer in the

Mold's Last Stand

If mold has gotten a foothold in your bathroom, you have several alternatives to combat it. Vinegar, hydrogen peroxide, oxygen bleach powder, borax, and tea tree oil have all been shown to kill it. Try the **Mildew and Germ Killer recipe on page 43**, or use your favorite nontoxic mold and mildew cleaner. Be sure to follow instructions—most nontoxic solutions require that you spray it on and let it sit because it needs time to do its work. A steam cleaner is also a great way to tackle mold. (See page 49 and Resources for more information.)

Once you've got the mold under control, spray your shower daily using a diluted vinegar solution to keep it from returning. Don't worry: the vinegar smell goes away as soon as it dries! Avoid using vinegar on tile walls, however, because acid can etch the tiles or grout. With tile, your best bets are prevention and frequent cleaning.

See page 68 for how to replace a bathroom vent fan that no longer works.

bathroom and in at least one other room in the house. Relative humidity levels should be kept below 50 percent. Use a dehumidifier, heater, or air-conditioner when other moisture controls fail.

· **Repair any leaks** in your bathroom and elsewhere in your house. Be aware that mold can grow inside your walls and ceiling. Any source of moisture will help mold thrive.

· **Let in sunlight and fresh air.** Sunlight kills mold, so use light-blocking blinds or curtains only when needed. When it's not humid outdoors, crack the window open to let in fresh air.

· **Extend shower curtains** fully after bathing so that there aren't folds where

moisture can lurk. Conversely, leave shower doors open so that air can circulate inside the stall.

· **Wipe down shower walls** after bathing, as outlined in "Preventing Soap Scum and Mold" on page 57.

· **Leave the bathroom door** open whenever possible so that air circulates from other parts of the house.

· **Hang up wet towels** and mats, preferably outside the bathroom, such as on a hook in the bedroom.

[smart tip]

Don't Scratch

Washing soda is more abrasive than borax or baking soda, so avoid using it on surfaces that scratch easily—especially fiberglass. Avoid other scouring powders on fiberglass as well.

Grout and Caulk

Grout is a classic difficult-to-clean area in your bathroom. Even if you kill any mold present, the grout may still be stained. Try the **Baking Soda Scrub recipe on page 44.** Spread it on the grout, scrub, and then rinse it with vinegar. (Don't use vinegar too often because it can dissolve grout.) A new, stiff-bristle toothbrush will help you scrub. (Notice I say a "new" toothbrush—I'm all for reusing items, but used toothbrushes are often so soft they are not good for scrubbing.) You may also consider sealing your grout with a nontoxic sealant. (See Resources.)

Caulk is used in joints, such as those where the shower walls meet the tub or where two acrylic shower panels meet. You can tell the difference because grout is rock hard, but caulk feels kind of rubbery. The worst situation is when the caulk shrinks or sags and the mold or grime is able to get behind the caulk. This makes it almost impossible to clean. Your only option is to replace the caulk.

Your best choice for a nontoxic caulk

Keep caulk lines neat by using painter's masking tape. Smooth caulk with a wet finger and then immediately remove the tape.

is one that is 100 percent silicone and does *not* specify use for kitchens or bathrooms. The kitchen and bath formulations sound attractive because they claim to inhibit mold, but they do so by impregnating the caulk with fungicides that may off-gas long after the caulk is applied.

FRESH AIR

Commercial air fresheners put lots of nasty chemicals in the air that you really don't want to breath. Both vinegar and baking soda have natural odor-killing properties. Combine them with essential oils, and you can leave the air clean and sweet smelling.

Use a fine-mist spray bottle filled with vinegar and several drops of the essential oil of your choice to combat odors wherever they occur. Or fill a decorative box or jar with baking soda mixed with a few drops of essential oil and leave it on a bathroom shelf. Scented baking soda can also be used in the bottom of kitchen garbage cans and diaper pails. If you like burning scented candles, you may want to try soy or beeswax ones that contain only essential oils for scent.

Add 5–10 drops of essential oil to your baking soda. Shake or mix the baking soda occasionally and add new drops of oil whenever the scent seems to have faded.

10 Ways to Fight Mold and Mildew

1. Keep your bathroom's humidity below 50 percent. Venting fans, heaters, dehumidifiers, and air-conditioners can all help lower humidity.

3. Hang a squeegee by the shower and leave the shower door open when it's not in use.

2. Keep caulk around sinks, faucets, and counters in good repair.

4. Install a venting fan.

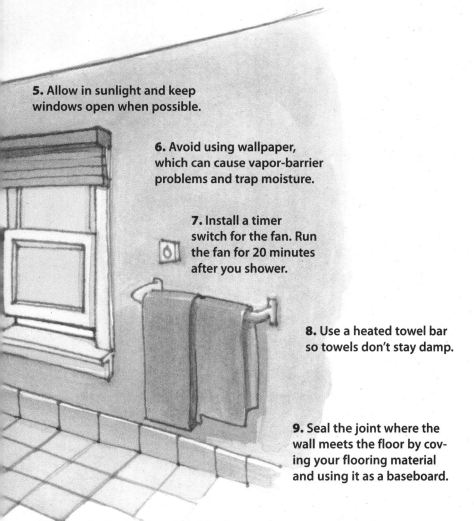

5. Allow in sunlight and keep windows open when possible.

6. Avoid using wallpaper, which can cause vapor-barrier problems and trap moisture.

7. Install a timer switch for the fan. Run the fan for 20 minutes after you shower.

8. Use a heated towel bar so towels don't stay damp.

9. Seal the joint where the wall meets the floor by coving your flooring material and using it as a baseboard.

10. Mop the floor regularly with vinegar. (To clean tile floors, use the **All-Purpose Liquid Cleaner on page 39.**)

REPLACE A VENT FAN

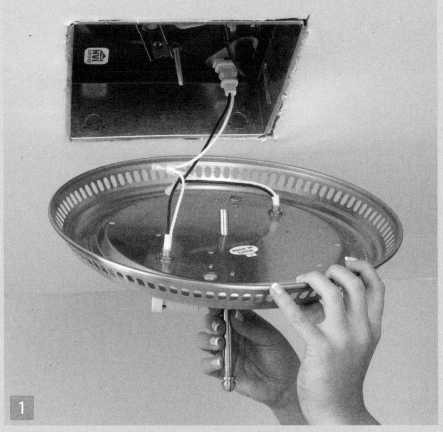

Replacing a faulty vent fan is a job most homeowners can tackle. Installing a unit where there was none is a bigger job and will likely involve the removal of portions of the ceiling drywall and running a new electrical line. Unless you have the skills, it is a job best left to a licensed electrician.

To remove the old housing, turn off the circuit, and loosen the clamps at the electrical cable and duct.

Trace the shape of the new housing, and cut away excess drywall.

Installing or replacing a malfunctioning bathroom fan will whisk away moist air that can otherwise cause assorted house problems, including mold growth. Begin by shutting off current to the fan at the circuit box. Then, reaching the old fan from the attic, if possible, remove the old unit. If you can't reach from above, remove it from below, and patch the ceiling later. Carefully detach the duct and electrical cable from the old fan housing.

Assemble and mount the new fan according to the manufacturer's instructions. Keep insulation 3 inches away from the fixture unless it is rated type IC, which is designed for such situations. Reattach the electrical cable and duct. Complete wiring connections, and attach ground wire. Install trim and, if your fan has a light, the fixture, appropriate bulb, and the translucent shield.

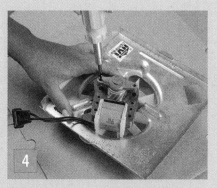

Assemble according to the manufacturer's directions. The motor plugs into an integral receptacle.

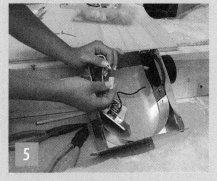

Use wire nuts and electrical tape to make wiring connections inside the wiring box, and mount to joist.

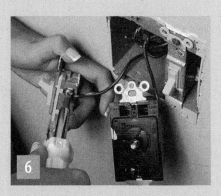

A timer switch allows your family to use the vent fan without worrying about turning it off.

It installs in place of a regular switch using the same electrical box and wires.

Staying on top of your cleaning chores is the key to not needing harsh cleaners. The toilet is no exception. Weekly (or even twice-weekly) cleaning will keep your toilet sparkling. The longer you allow grime to build, the stronger the cleaner you'll need to remove it. Before using the methods on the opposite page, be sure to remove any auto-

Toilet Exteriors

The outside of your toilet is actually more likely to be a haven for bacteria than the bowl because the bowl is rinsed with fresh water every time you flush. Use the **Glass Cleaner on page 40** to clean and disinfect at the same time. (Studies have shown that vinegar kills 99 percent of all bacteria it contacts.)

Regular Toilet Cleaning

Spray with the **Glass Cleaner on page 40;** scrub the bowl, getting under the rim; and flush. This should do it if you clean regularly. For moderate and stubborn stains, see the methods on the opposite page.

matic toilet-bowl cleaners from your reservoir tank and rinse the toilet brush thoroughly to remove any chemical residue, which can react with your new cleaners.

Keep your toilet brush from growing mold or bacteria between cleanings by spraying it with vinegar or a tea tree oil solution after each use. When possible, leave the brush out to dry completely before putting it back in its holder.

Green Fact

Approximately 25 million Americans suffer from allergic reactions to mold. Exposure to mold in damp homes can double the risk of asthma development in children. Mold spores can start sprouting as quickly as 24 hours after an area becomes damp.

Removing Moderate Stains

What you'll need: borax, hot water, liquid castile soap, toilet brush, and a spray bottle

*Drop the water level before cleaning by either 1) turning off the shutoff valve (usually located down behind the toilet), and then flushing or 2) using a plunger or a special toilet brush called a "johnny mop" to force some of the water out the bottom of the bowl. Then, using the **All-Surface Spray on page 38,** apply a generous amount around the toilet bowl and under the rim, using a toilet brush. Let it sit for five minutes; scrub again; and then flush.*

Removing Stubborn Stains

What you'll need: pumice stone

For stubborn mineral deposits, you may have to resort to scrubbing with a pumice stone. Pumice stones are often used to smooth calluses on feet, so look for them in the skin-care section at the pharmacy. Soak the pumice before using it to avoid scratching the porcelain. Drop the water level in the toilet; scrub stains using the pumice; and then flush.

Use an abrasive pumice stone to clean away the toughest mineral stains.

Soak your pumice stone in water for 15 minutes before using.

Conventional drain cleaners are some of the most toxic substances you can have in your home. They are highly corrosive and can produce dangerous fumes. For 2005, the American Association of Poison Control Centers reported that seven people died of exposure to drain cleaners, 60 ended up with a significant disability or disfigurement, and more than 600 had pronounced symptoms that needed treatment. Do yourself a favor and take these substances to your hazardous-waste collection site.

When Clogs Occur

There are several ways to deal with clogged drains, and most of them work

Preventing Clogs

As is the case with most cleaning problems, spending a little time on prevention is well worth the effort. Trust me, there is never a good time to have a clogged drain, and in my experience it is most likely to happen just before guests arrive! Try the methods on these two pages to keep your drains free of clogs.

as well or even better than commercial drain cleaners. If the shower or tub drain is clogged, remove the drain cover, and pull out as much hair or debris as possible. Then try the methods on these pages.

Clearing Drains

It's often enough to fill a sink or tub with water and then release the stopper to clear clogged drains. The water pressure will frequently dislodge the clog, especially if you attack the problem before the drain is completely closed. Help the process along by cupping your hand over the open drain as you release the stopper and use it as you would a plunger.

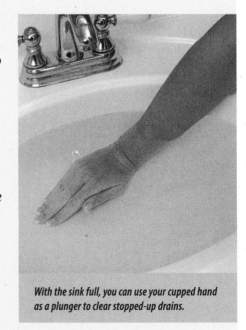

With the sink full, you can use your cupped hand as a plunger to clear stopped-up drains.

Safety Note: *do not use any of these methods with a commercial drain cleaner. It could splash out and burn you or mix with other chemicals to create dangerous fumes.*

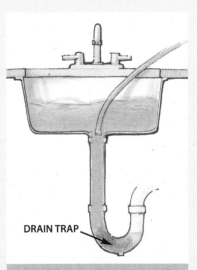

Use a Hair Catcher

Hair catchers on shower drains don't work perfectly, but they do catch a lot more hair than the huge holes in most drain covers.

Clearing Partially Clogged Drains

What you'll need: plunger and rags

Make sure there is some water in the drain. Then block the overflow drain (if any) using a wet rag, and press down firmly. With the plunger against the drain to form an airtight seal, push down, and then pull up. Repeat until water starts to drain or proceed to the next method.

Clearing Tough Clogs

What you'll need: hose connected to nearby spigot

If the drain is completely clogged, run a hose from an outdoor or indoor spigot. Remove any sprayer attachment; hold the hose in the drain hole; and have someone turn on the water full blast. The rush of water should break up the clog.

DRAIN TRAP

The water pressure from a hose is usually enough to clear any local obstruction. Don't use this method if you suspect an obstruction beyond the trap.

smart tip

Kitchen Detox

It has often been said that the kitchen is the heart of the home. And as we all know, the heart is essential to the functioning of the entire body. So it follows that the kitchen should be the first place from which you remove toxins.

I found that greening up the kitchen is pretty easy. Just switch to a nontoxic all-surface spray and dish soap and you're pretty much set. The only tricky part is disinfecting surfaces, but there are plenty of strategies you can use, from microwaving sponges to spraying vinegar and hydrogen peroxide. Be sure to switch to a nontoxic dishwasher soap too—my homemade recipe works great and you'll only find it here!

Keep kitchen cleaning tools and appliances spotless. Boil sponges to disinfect them, left. Dust cabinets regularly, right, and use dish-washing liquid to remove grease. You'll be surprised at how well these methods work!

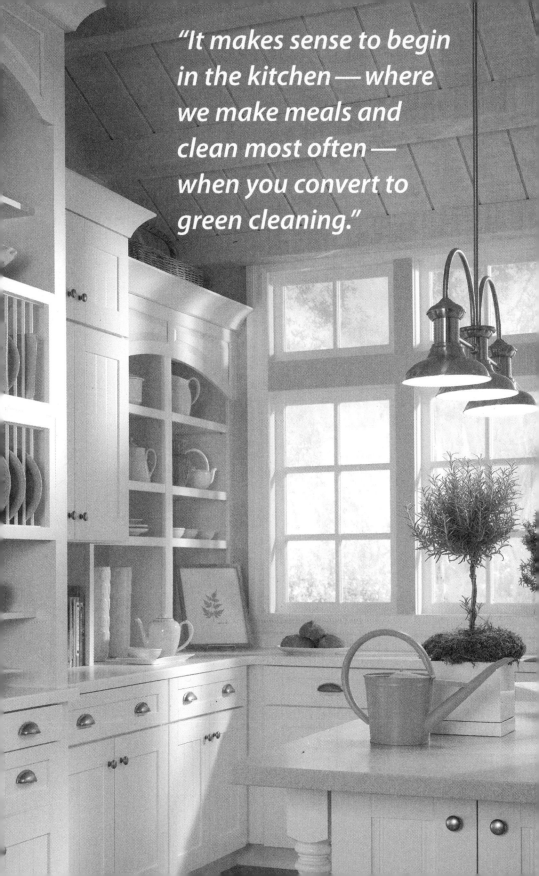

"It makes sense to begin in the kitchen — where we make meals and clean most often — when you convert to green cleaning."

Most sinks and countertops can be cleaned using the methods described below. Some surfaces are sensitive to acid, so wipe up acidic spills quickly, and use acidic cleaners, such as lemon juice or vinegar, with care. Most surfaces can't stand up to harsh abrasives either, so stick to soft cleansers and sponges.

Special Surface Considerations

Solid-surfacing material and plastic laminate: Dark or glossy surfaces, especially, show scratches easily, so be careful not to use any abrasives on them. However, they are less likely than wood, stone, and tile countertops to support the growth of bacteria.

Clean Everyday Spills and Stains

What you'll need: hand-dishwashing liquid and water

*For everyday cleaning, use a hand-dishwashing liquid and water, or the **All-Surface Spray on page 38.***

Clean Moderate Stains

What you'll need: baking soda and water

Make a paste of baking soda and water; spread it over the stain; let it sit for 10 minutes; and then wipe. Rinse well.

Oxygen bleach uses hydrogen peroxide or sodium percarbonate to lift stains.

Clean Stubborn Stains

What you'll need: oxygen bleach powder and hot water

If baking soda doesn't work, try a paste made with oxygen-bleach powder and hot water. Spread it over the stain; wait 30 minutes (or as directed); and then rinse.

Most countertops cannot stand up to abrasive cleansers, but you can keep the surface clean and free of bacteria without using harsh chemicals.

Tile: To remove ground-in dirt from grout, try the **Baking Soda Scrub on page 44.** Let it sit for 10 minutes; scrub again; and then spray with vinegar and rinse immediately with water. Or try a paste made with oxygen-bleach powder and water.

Stainless steel and chrome: To remove water spots, spray with club soda or vinegar, and polish with a soft cloth until it is completely dry. Use fresh lemon juice to remove rust stains. (Let it sit for several hours.) Salt and bleach can both damage stainless steel.

Butcher block: To remove stains, make a paste of salt and fresh lemon juice, rub it into the stain, let it sit overnight, and then rinse. When oiling your wood counters, bowls, or cutting boards, use raw food-grade linseed oil (also called flax seed oil). Avoid boiled linseed oil, which usually has toxic

Disinfecting Food-Prep Areas

Spray surfaces generously with the **Mildew and Germ Killer on page 43.** Allow to sit at least 15 minutes.

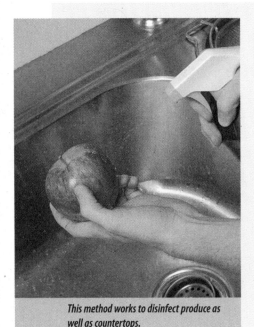

This method works to disinfect produce as well as countertops.

Disinfectant Alternative

What you'll need: white vinegar, hydrogen peroxide, and a spray bottle

Spray the surface with white vinegar and follow immediately with hydrogen peroxide (the 3-percent solution you can find in the pharmacy). The hydrogen peroxide spray bottle needs to be opaque to protect it from light, so you may simply want to screw on a spray nozzle to the original bottle. Do not mix vinegar and hydrogen peroxide in the same bottle.

Integral drain boards, single-lever faucets, and built-in soap dispensers give bacteria fewer places to hide.

chemicals in it to help speed the drying process. Walnut oil also works well.

Stone: Vinegar and other acids will ruin stone, so avoid them at all costs.

Food-Prep Areas

Given the bacteria that can be present with raw meat and produce, it makes sense to take extra care with food-preparation areas. Scrubbing a surface with hot, soapy water and then letting it dry completely will get rid of most germs. Areas that you need to be most concerned about are those that are scratched, those with nooks and crannies that you can't thoroughly clean, and those that stay damp from frequent use. On these types of surfaces, try the cleaning methods on the opposite page. Note that preliminary research indicates that these ingredients are effective, but they have not been recognized yet by the EPA as disinfectants. One herbal disinfectant that has been registered with the EPA is Benefect. (See Resources.)

Sponges, Dishcloths, and More

Disinfect sponges by boiling them in a pot of water for five minutes or microwave them on high for one minute. (Be sure they are wet because the sponges must be *boiled*.) Dishcloths can be boiled, laundered, or microwaved wet for three minutes. Scrub brushes and scouring pads can be boiled or run through the dishwasher. Don't run sponges through the dishwasher, however. Studies have shown that this method does not get them entirely clean.

A well-organized kitchen makes tasks easier, and it's less work to keep clean.

CHAPTER 4 **KITCHEN DETOX**

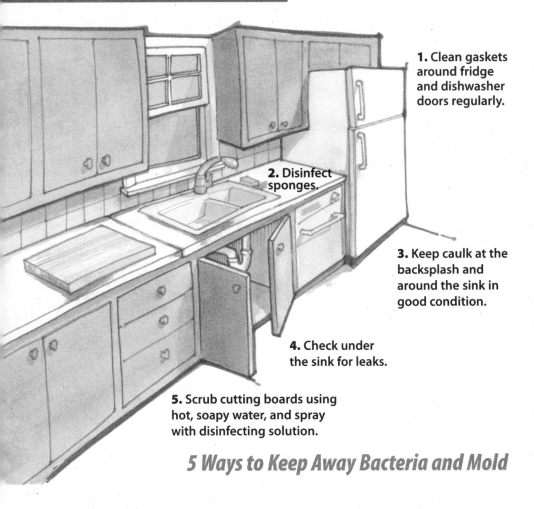

1. Clean gaskets around fridge and dishwasher doors regularly.

2. Disinfect sponges.

3. Keep caulk at the backsplash and around the sink in good condition.

4. Check under the sink for leaks.

5. Scrub cutting boards using hot, soapy water, and spray with disinfecting solution.

5 Ways to Keep Away Bacteria and Mold

BACTERIA CENTRAL

Your sponge or dishcloth is probably the most contaminated item in your entire house because it provides a warm, moist environment for bacteria to grow. When you use it to clean, you spread the bacteria throughout your kitchen—ick! The key is to disinfect it frequently and allow it to dry completely between uses. Dishcloths are a better choice because they dry faster. If you buy a dozen dishcloths, you can use a new one every day, and then just wash the dirty ones with the rest of your laundry.

The top five spots for bacteria contamination in your home are as follows:

1. Kitchen sponges and dishcloths
2. Kitchen sink
3. Bathroom sink
4. Cutting boards
5. Kitchen floor

Cutting Boards

Plastic or wooden cutting boards are both fine as long as you care for them properly. Once a plastic cutting board gets scratched, plain scrubbing with soap and water won't get out all the germs—run it through the dishwasher or soak it with a disinfectant solution to get it clean. Or get rid of it. Scratched wooden boards have an advantage because scrubbing still gets their surface clean, but some bacteria can get sucked down into the wood's pores. I spray mine with tea tree oil every few days.

Cabinet pulls that keep fingers off the woodwork will save hours of scrubbing. Select a style that's also easy to remove, just in case.

Green Fact

According to the U.S. Department of Energy, prerinsing your dishes can use up to 20 gallons of water. Energy Star dishwashers, which typically use one-third less water than nonqualified models, are designed to do the cleaning so you don't have to prerinse.

CABINETRY

Dusting your kitchen cabinets frequently will help prevent the dust and grease from combining into a tough-to-clean goo. Your hand-dishwashing soap or any mild liquid soap is fine for routine cleaning—don't soak the surface, just wipe it using a damp cloth or sponge. Be sure to dilute your liquid soap sufficiently so that you don't have to use a lot of water to rinse.

The areas around the handles get dirty fastest, so pay special attention to them. Grease is the biggest culprit when it comes to dirty cabinets, so always use your exhaust hood whenever you cook to minimize the splatters. For information on polishing and waxing your wood cabinets, see the wood furniture care tips on page 148.

Wiping Away Grease

For heavy grease buildup, look for a nontoxic brand cleaner that uses citrus as a degreaser. Citrus solvents are part of the terpene family, and the active ingredient is called d-limonene. Use them sparingly and only with good ventilation because they contain VOCs that can irritate your lungs.

You may also find it easiest to remove the pulls or handles for this job. It's a lot easier than trying to scrub under and around the hardware. Removing one or two screws is all it takes. Test all cleaners and solvent on a small area before proceeding to the rest of the cabinet.

I've found that club soda is the best for cleaning the surfaces of appliances. Be sure to buy the regular kind—not "reduced sodium" or it won't work as well. Just put it in a spray bottle; spritz the appliance; and let it sit for a few seconds, and then wipe it. Be sure to wipe thoroughly in order to avoid leaving spots or streaks. It works particularly well with microfiber cloths, available in many weaves at your supermarket.

Microwaves

Use a microwave plate cover or paper towel to prevent splatters. Wipe the cover after each use, and run it through the dishwasher as needed. When grime builds, boil a cup of vinegar in the microwave for five minutes, and then let it sit for several minutes. The steam from the vinegar will loosen the grime.

Ovens

If you have a self-cleaning oven, take advantage of the cleaning cycle on a regular basis. Don't wait for a thick layer of grime to amass. If you use it this way, the cleaning cycle does a good job, and you shouldn't ever have to scrub. If your oven isn't self-cleaning (or if you'd prefer to use less electricity), baking soda is an easy solution. Simply make a paste with water, and spread it thickly over the walls and bottom of the oven. Let it sit overnight. The next day the grime should be soft enough to scrape. Steam cleaning also works great.

Whenever possible, use covers or foil on your dishes. When a spill occurs during cooking, pour salt on it to absorb the liquid and stop it from smoking. You will be able to remove the spill the next day with ease. Wipe down your oven after each use, while it is still warm (but not hot). Never use commercial oven cleaners—not only are they highly toxic, but they also may damage self-cleaning or continuous-cleaning ovens.

Apply water and baking-soda paste to a dirty oven and allow it to remain overnight.

Stoves

Smooth-top glass and ceramic stoves should be treated similarly to countertops. (See page 76.) Wipe spills immediately and never use anything abrasive. For tough stains, make a paste of baking soda and dish soap, and cover the stain for 10 minutes. Always use a freshly washed dishcloth or sponge, and don't leave streaks or a haze on the cooktop. Any residue left over from cleaning may turn yellow the next time you use the appliance.

To keep both gas and electric stoves and cooktops clean, wipe with a damp rag or sponge and soapy water after each use. Occasionally soak removable parts (such as the burner drip plates and control knobs) in soapy water, or run them through the dishwasher if your owner's manual says that they are dishwasher safe.

KITCHENWARE

Nontoxic hand-dishwashing liquids are easy to find even at your local grocery store these days. Most of them work just as well as their conventional competitors, so experiment with a few and pick one you like. Avoid ones that say "antibacterial"—antibacterial agents may help create antibiotic-resistant "superbugs," and the American Medical Association advises against them. To keep things really simple, just use a liquid castile soap, which I recommend for many other uses in this book as well.

It is a bit more problematic to find a nontoxic automatic dishwasher detergent that works well for everyone. It depends on both the type of water and the dishwasher. I'm happy to say that after trying many formulas that did not work, I have found a homemade recipe that performs well for me. **(See Dishwasher**

[smart tip]

Coffeemaker Cleansing

Run vinegar through your coffeemaker regularly to clean it and remove calcium buildup. Scrub the coffeepot with a paste made of baking soda and water, or one made of salt and lemon juice.

Laundry isn't the only thing you can hang to dry. Air-dry pots and pans over the sink.

Powder on page 41.) If you prefer to purchase a store-bought product, look for one that is chlorine- and phosphate-free. (Automatic dishwasher detergents are the only products that are still allowed to contain phosphates.) Try using half the amount of detergent recommended by the manufacturer—you'd be surprised how little you actually need to do the job.

Pots and Pans

Have I mentioned how much I love baking soda? Keep some in a shaker can near your sink. If you use a dish or pan but aren't going to have time to wash it immediately, rinse it with water, and then sprinkle it with baking soda. This will keep the food particles from hardening. For heavy-duty jobs, soak the pan for several hours in hot water with a few tablespoons of baking soda—you may even want to put it on the stove and boil it gently for several minutes.

Pullouts should be easy to reach while prepping meals, and trash bins should be easy to remove for cleaning.

Glasses

When you're hand washing dinner-ware, always wash glasses first to avoid getting grease on them. Dry them thoroughly by hand if you want to be sure to avoid spotting. If your glasses come out of the dishwasher looking cloudy, try putting vinegar in the rinse agent dispenser occasionally.

Kitchen Cleaning Tools

A dishcloth is a better choice than a sponge because it dries quicker and allows less chance for bacteria to grow. (See "Bacteria Central" on page 82 for more information.)

For more scrubbing power, try a microfiber "waffle weave" dishcloth. It's amazing how effective they are, and how they release accumulated

"Detergent residue remains on dishes after they are washed and gets in you food. I've switched to my own recipe of just borax and citric acid and it works great. **See the recipe on page 41.**" – J.S.

DISHWASHING DEBATE

There is a continued controversy over what is better for the environment: to hand wash your dishes or to use a dishwasher. The answer is, it depends. A dishwasher probably uses less water if you don't rinse your dishes in the sink beforehand, you only run it when it is full, and you use a low-energy cycle. But if you prerinse, then you might as well wash by hand.

However, you can conserve water even if you wash dishes by hand. Fill a plastic bucket with hot, soapy water for washing. Then use a second bucket filled with clear, hot water for rinsing.

Surprisingly, dishwashers also seem to use less energy, presumably because they use so much less hot water than the average hand-washer. But if you factor in the life cycle of the dishwasher and the energy needed to manufacture it and then to recycle it when its usefulness is done, then hand washing comes out ahead.

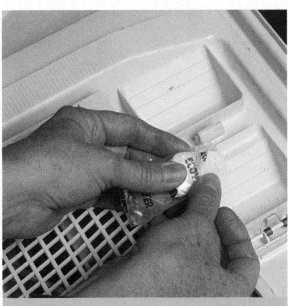

If you do use the dishwasher, choose a plant-based detergent.

soil when rinsed. Keep one for spot cleaning your floor, too. Natural-bristle scrub brushes are the best from an environmental point of view, but I admit I tend to use plastic-bristle brushes because they hold up longer. You can also use the nylon mesh bags used for onions and potatoes. Don't forget a wooden or plastic scraper—getting off as much food as possible from your dishes before you wash them makes the whole process much easier.

Silverware

The simplest way to avoid noxious silverware polish is to use stainless-steel flatware. But if you have a taste for the finer things in life, there are some surprisingly simple ways to keep your silverware shining. The method described below will brighten silver in minutes. The electrolytic process literally lifts the tarnish from the utensils. This method is particularly good for silverware with intricate patterns that are difficult to hand polish. Use this method outside or in a room with the windows open. The chemical reaction releases hydrogen sulfide gas, smells like rotten eggs, and is not good to inhale. If you don't mind polishing piece by piece, sprinkle baking soda on a damp cloth and rub until the tarnish is removed. Never use rubber gloves while polishing because it is corrosive to silver.

MAKE SILVERWARE SHINE

Place a sheet of aluminum foil at the bottom of a glass-proof baking dish, and then lay the silver plate on top.

Sprinkle one teaspoon of salt and several tablespoons of baking soda over the silver-plated dinnerware.

Scraping off burned foods from your frying pan makes washing easier.

3

Pour boiling water over the silver plate. There will be a bubbling action for about half a minute.

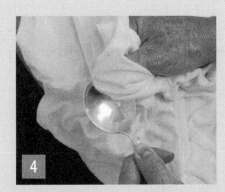
4

Remove each piece and polish with a soft cloth, such as an old cotton T-shirt.

Laundry You Can Live With

Laundry never used to be a top priority for me, but since I became a mom it's taken on new importance. It seems I am always washing something, from cloth diapers to cleaning rags to toddler clothes.

As the number of washes I did grew, I searched for ways to lessen my impact. I line-dry as much as possible, but I have to dry clothes indoors because I have pollen allergies. I make sure I use the most economical settings on my washer and dryer, and a front-loading washing machine is on my wish list. One thing I've worked hard to get better at is treating stains. It's easier to treat stains when they're fresh; it helps clothes look nicer longer, and I can often just treat a stain and wear the item again instead of filling up the laundry basket.

Clothes-drying racks come in many types, including the indoor unit, left. Hang laundry outdoors for fresh, summer-scented laundry, right.

"There are plenty of ways to green up your laundry... including some time-honored ones."

Reduce your energy and water consumption by using the following tips:

• **Only wash your clothes when they are dirty.** If they still look and smell clean when you take them off, put them back in your closet.

• **Get in the habit of treating stains immediately.** The longer you wait, the stronger the chemical you'll need to remove the stain—and it may not come out at all.

• **Run your washing machine only when it's full.** If you do run half a load, adjust the water level to match if your washer has this feature.

• **Don't overload your washer.** Clothes need room to agitate; otherwise, they won't come out clean. Front-loading washers agitate more effectively.

• **Know how long your wash cycle is and set a timer** so you don't forget to dry the clothes. Wet clothes get musty fast and then must be rewashed.

• **Use cold water to wash your clothes whenever possible**—a lot of energy is wasted heating water, and many detergents work just fine in cold water. Always use a cold rinse.

• **Spot wash and wear.** If you spill something on a clean shirt, don't just throw it in the hamper—spot wash it, and hang it to dry so you can wear it again.

• **Use nontoxic laundry products** (see page 98) and try using half the amount of detergent recommended.

"I try to line-dry at least half my clothes. In the summer, it really gives my dryer a break. In the winter, I hang them on a rack in the bedroom. They're out of sight there, and the moisture humidifies the dry air." – J. S.

CHOOSING A WASHER AND DRYER

When buying a new washer, your first decision is top-loading or front-loading. Front loaders are relatively new in the United States, but they've been common in Europe for years. They have several advantages: they use less water and less energy; they are gentler on clothes; and their high-speed spin cycle extracts more water, which cuts down on drying time.

However, front-loading models are harder on your back because you have to bend over to load and unload them; they require special "high-efficinecy" low-sudsing detergents; you can't soak a whole load of clothes (it only fills with water halfway); and they are significantly more expensive. Some people have complained about mold growing inside front- loading washers. So do your homework before you buy one, and make sure you always leave the door open so the interior can dry completely between washes.

Despite these drawbacks, I feel front-loading machines are still the better choice from an environmental point of view.

As for dryers, choose one that runs on propane or natural gas and you will contribute 60 percent less carbon dioxide to the air than if you used an electric dryer. A gas-dryer's annual operating costs are usually less as well. If your town does not offer gas hookup, you can have a tank installed. Be sure to select a model with moisture sensors, which shut down the dryer when clothes are dry. This protects clothes, saves energy, and helps prevent dryer fires.

Always look for Energy Star rated appliances, too.

Front-loading washers conserve water. They also use less energy because they spin more water out of clothes and reduce drying times.

You can also make changes to the way you dry laundry—even if you use a clothes dryer.

• **Use the moisture sensor setting** on

Solar Clothes Drying

Dry clothes on a drying rack or clothesline. There are an amazing amount of drying-rack options available now that don't take up much space. Clothes dried outdoors smell great. Clothes dried indoors help humidify dry air.

your dryer to prevent over-drying.

• **Remove lint** from your dryer's filter every time you use it; otherwise, it will work hotter and harder and use more energy. Lint is also a fire hazard.

• **Avoid commercial fabric softeners** (both liquids and dryer sheets)—they are toxic. Use vinegar instead.

• **Dry only full loads.** The tumbling action needed to dry clothes efficiently works best when the dryer is full but not over-full. If you need to dry just a few items, throw a couple of dry towels in with them.

WHAT ABOUT DRY CLEANING?

Most dry-cleaning facilities in the United States use the solvent perchloroethylene ("perc" for short). I don't have room to list all the ways this stuff is toxic. Chronic exposure can cause damage to the nervous system, liver, and kidneys. The EPA lists it as a potential carcinogen and a hazardous air pollutant. In short, don't let your clothes get near the stuff.

Your alternatives? Well, you can try hand washing your "dry clean only" garments in cold water with a mild soap or detergent and then lying them

flat to air dry. This is a gamble, though, because hand washing may damage the fabric or cause shrinkage or color loss.

If you use a dry cleaner, there are three new types of dry-cleaning solvents that are billed as much less toxic. They are liquid carbon dioxide, silicone-based cleaning, and "wet cleaning," which uses a tiny amount of water. (See Resources for more information.) From what I've learned, they work pretty well and are more environmentally friendly. But like any new technology, it

may be years before we know if these solvents pose any health risks.

If you do use a conventional dry cleaner, remember: your garment shouldn't have a strong chemical smell after it is cleaned. If it does, it means the solvent hasn't completely evaporated—take it back to the cleaners and ask them to dry it more thoroughly. In any case, take it out of the bag when you get home and air it outdoors or in your garage for several days before putting it in your closet.

ECO CLOTHING CARE

Manufacturing clothes uses energy and resources, so the longer you make yours last, the less adverse environmental impact they have.

• **Close zippers and hook and loop tape and empty pockets** before washing clothes to prevent snags and stains.

• **Wash clothing inside out**—especially fuzzy fabrics such as fleece or chenille that tend to pick up lint.

• **Put delicates in a lingerie bag** to prevent them from getting damaged during the washing process.

• **Always air-dry delicate fabrics** such as silk, linen, and rayon, even if the tag says they can be put in the clothes dryer.

• **Sort your clothes.** Dark and bright-colored clothes almost always bleed tiny amounts of dye during washing, and they will make your light colors look dingy in no time fast.

• **Get kids in the habit of changing** into play clothes when they get home from school.

[smart tip]

Not All or Nothing

You don't have to give up your clothes dryer entirely. Even if you only hang your clothes to line dry once a week, or just during the summer, you'll still be making a significant difference.

[smart *tip*]

Banishing Wrinkles

To avoid wrinkles, use the permanent press cycle for synthetic fabrics, always remove clothes as soon as they are dry, and fold or hang them. Don't overload the dryer. Don't overdry your clothes.

bly cutting costs and did not preshrink the fabric or use color-fast dyes.

• **Avoid clothes** that need ironing or dry cleaning.

• **Choose dark colors over white or light-color clothes**—whites take a lot more effort to keep clean looking. Limit them to special occasions. (I will never understand why white socks are the standard!)

• **Designate a spot** in your closet for stained or damaged clothes that can be used as work clothes for dirty chores. When you've worn them all you can, cut them up and make rags.

• **Buy high-quality clothes** (preferably organic) that are built to last. Avoid cotton clothes that say "wash separately" or "cold water wash only" because this indicates the manufacturer was proba-

Avoid Permanent Press

Avoid fabrics labeled "permanent press," "stain resistant," or "wrinkle resistant" because, most likely, they are treated with chemicals that are not good for you. Stick to natural, untreated fibers.

THE GREEN ALTERNATIVES

Your washing supplies don't need to be a toxic stew. Store-bought nontoxic products are getting better. Check out some of the following options:

Laundry detergent: There are plenty of nontoxic detergents. As with automatic dishwasher detergent, you may need to experiment with several brands before you find one you like. Everyone's water, washing machine, and personal preferences are different. **On page 42 I share my Laundry Soap recipe** and offer tips on what ingredients to avoid in store-bought products. (See Resources, page 218, for eco-friendly brands you might want to check.)

Fabric softener: White vinegar works wonderfully as a fabric softener. It helps prevent static cling, too. Use ¼ cup in the rinse cycle (never the wash cycle!) of

Washing machines, which last an average of about nine years, are responsible for about 22 percent of household water consumption—the equivalent of approximately 13,000 gallons of water each year—according to the American Water Works Association Research Foundation.

every load. The vinegar smell won't linger in your clothes. If you want to add a little fragrance, you can add a couple drops of your favorite essential oil. Once you find a scent you like, you can add about 50 drops ($\frac{1}{2}$ teaspoon) to each gallon of vinegar.

Bleach alternatives: My husband had a hard time giving up chlorine bleach, but I changed his mind with a new secret weapon: oxygen bleach. It works great and it's actually just a mix of hydrogen peroxide and washing soda. Oxygen bleach has been around for years in "non-chlorine" bleaches. Now many eco-brands (see Resources) offer it in a highly concentrated form without all the nasty additives that come with conventional non-chlorine bleaches.

Add it to your white loads regularly to

[smart tip]

Buy Locally

Laundry detergent is heavy, which makes it really expensive to order by mail. If you don't make your own, try to get your local grocery or health-food store to carry an eco-friendly brand for you. Give the store the brand information, and then call the manufacturer's headquarters and give them your local store's information, too.

When installing a laundry, choose a warm interior location. It will help save on energy costs when using an automatic dryer—and it will be more comfortable for you!

keep them looking white. (The amount you need will vary by brand, so read your label.) It's best to let your laundry soak in the oxygen bleach before adding soap and starting the wash cycle. It's also a great stain remover. Don't use it on silk or wool, though, because it may damage the fabric. And always test in an inconspicuous spot first.

Don't have any oxygen bleach on hand? Lemon juice is a whitener, too. Squeeze 1/4 cup of lemon juice and put it in your wash cycle. Or soak your garment with several tablespoons of lemon juice in a gallon of water. For

Hand Washables

Silk, wool, and other delicate fibers need special care. Wash them in cold water with a small amount of liquid castile soap. Gently swirl them in the water and rinse thoroughly. Don't wring them out—a good way to remove some water is to roll them in a clean bath towel. Always air-dry.

the best results, hang it in the sun to dry—sunlight is a natural bleach.

Baby Laundry

For baby laundry it is especially important to select a product that is not only mild but fragrance-free because fragrance is one of the top skin irritants. As I mentioned in Chapter 1, my son is allergic to detergents, and I believe that it is the root of many cases of infant eczema. I encourage everyone with children to use soap-based, rather than detergent-based, laundry products. When in doubt, use an extra rinse to free clothing of residue. (See Resources for makers of pure soap products.)

Laundry Balls

Avoid laundry balls and discs that claim you can wash your clothes without any chemicals. It sounds ideal, but I've yet to find any reputable source that says they work any better than plain water alone. Because most people use way too much detergent, the balls may appear to work at first because the clothes look cleaner without all that detergent residue. I've read that dryer balls used as fabric softeners do work, but they are made out of PVC, a plastic you want to avoid.

Use a mild, fragrance-free soap for baby's laundry.

Got stains? Try the following tips:

• **Never rub a fresh stain**—gently blot with a white cloth or paper towel.

• **Rinse protein stains** (egg, milk, urine, feces, vomit, blood, and so forth) under cold running water while scrubbing

gently. If the stain doesn't come right out, soak it in cold water. (Always make sure it's cold because warm or hot water can "cook" the protein and make the stain permanent.) If this doesn't work, try hydrogen peroxide on protein stains—it works well on blood stains.

• **Pretreat oil-based stains** (cooking oil, food grease, motor oil) by applying a liquid soap or detergent directly to the stain and rubbing gently. Rinse with hot water, and then wash with hot water.

• **Soak tannin stains** (red wine, coffee, tea, juice, ketchup, soft drinks, and so forth) for 30 minutes with 1 teaspoon liquid detergent per ½ gallon water. The oils in soap can set these stains, so detergent, or plain washing soda, is better in this instance.

Green Fact

Commercial stain removers often include a host of nasty ingredients, including nerve-damaging neuro-toxins, such as benzene tolune and xylene, as well as the carcinogen, formaldehyde. Stain removers made from plant oils are effective on all types of stains and are far better for you and the environment.

Cloth Diapers

Today's cloth diapers are adorable and easy to use (no folding or pins!). They are better for your child's health (conventional disposables use a lot of chemicals), save you money, and contribute a lot less waste to landfills. However, washing them uses a lot of water.

Never use fabric softener or chlorine bleach with cloth diapers. Most people will tell you to use detergents, not soaps, because the soap can build up on the diapers. I believe as long as you use washing soda in the wash and vinegar in the rinse you can prevent (or at least greatly minimize) this.

To wash cloth diapers, first do a *cold wash* with no soap or detergent and a cold rinse with ¼ cup vinegar. Next, soak them in hot water with oxygen bleach to whiten them and kill germs. Then wash according to my **Laundry Soap recipe on page 42.**

Today's cloth diapers are easy to use, save you money, and cut way back on trash.

Around the House

Next up on our to-do list are walls and ceilings, as well as other interior jobs, such as cleaning metal and dusting. When it comes to this cleaning, I tend to procrastinate. After all, these surfaces don't get dirty fast—it can be months before it really starts to show. But as I've stressed over and over again, being proactive is an important green cleaning tactic because it usually uses fewer resources and energy in the long run.

One chore that everyone likes to procrastinate is cleaning windows. However, the squeegee method outlined in this chapter may change your attitude. This is a commercial window-cleaning technique that I found adapts beautifully to green cleaning. I love it when something is quick, easy, *and* green.

Steam cleaners make fast work of cleaning windows, left and right—no chemicals needed. If you want to go more low-tech, a squeegee and a bucket with some eco-friendly cleaning solution will also get the job done easily.

"Windows, walls, and ceilings all lend themselves well to a green makeover."

It's amazing the difference clean windows can make. After I had my son, I let my living room windows go a long time without cleaning. When I finally got to them I couldn't believe what a facelift clean windows gave the whole room. Fortunately, glass is one of the easiest surfaces to clean in a nontoxic and eco-friendly manner.

Your average bottle of "blue stuff" may seem pretty harmless, but most of those bottles have ammonia in them. And because glass cleaner is almost always a spray-on solution, there isn't any way to avoid breathing it into your lungs. Try the alternatives below instead.

Windows

Most conventional glass cleaners include wax that leaves a thin coat on the windows, supposedly so that dirt won't stick to the glass and stays cleaner longer. The first couple of times you clean your windows with a nontoxic cleaner, you will need to remove this wax. Use either a store-bought brand that has a surfactant in it, or add soap to your homemade cleaner. **(See the Glass Cleaner recipe on page 40.)** A microfiber cloth also helps scrub off the wax. After the first few times, you can use just vinegar and water.

Sprayed-on club soda also works well. Here are a few tips for cleaning windows:

- **Clean windowsills and frames** before starting to wash the glass.
- **Don't clean** windows in direct sun—they dry too quickly and leave streaks.
- **Use a squeegee** instead of paper towels to save resources.
- **Start at the top** and work your way down the window.
- **Vacuum window screens** in place using a soft dust-brush attachment. Remove extra-dirty screens and hose them. Then use a soft brush to gently remove the dirt.

Easy-to-operate windows are important to a green-clean house because sunlight and air circulation are essential to combating mold and indoor air pollutants.

JUST SQUEEGEE IT!

When you're doing a full cleaning of all the windows in your home, don't use a spray bottle and paper towels. Save time and effort by using a sponge and a squeegee.

1. Grab two buckets. Fill one with one part water, one part vinegar, and a few drops of liquid soap or dish detergent. Fill the other bucket with plain water.

2. Take a large sponge or soft scrub brush, dip it in the soapy bucket, wring it, and scrub the window thoroughly. Use a very wet steel-wool pad to remove any stubborn spots.

Scrub the window with a sponge and soapy water. Use wet steel wool or a razor blade to remove any spots that you cannot remove with the sponge.

3. Take your squeegee (preferably a 12-inch-wide one with a very soft rubber blade) and run it across the top of the window from left to right.

4. Wipe off your squeegee with a clean cloth or sponge. (It is important to keep the blade clean to avoid streaks.) Then, starting on one side, pull the squeegee down the window until you get about 3 inches from the bottom of the window.

5. Wipe the squeegee blade, again, and repeat steps 2 and 3, working your way across the window, overlapping your last path slightly each time.

6. Run your squeegee across the bottom of the window. Then use a sponge or rag to mop up any water that is left at the bottom of the window.

7. Rinse out your large sponge in the clean bucket of water, dip it in the soapy bucket, and start on the next window. Replace the water in the bucket as often as needed to keep it clean.

Keep the edge of the squeegee blade firmly against the window and pull it downward in a straight line.

Run your squeegee across the bottom of the window, and then use a sponge or rag to wipe off the sill.

The three biggest offenders when it comes to dirty walls and ceilings are: 1) smoke from cigarettes, candles, fireplaces, or wood stoves; 2) grease from a kitchen stove; and 3) kids. To minimize collecting dirt, try the following prevention strategies:

• **Do not allow smoking** inside the house.

• **Perform proper maintenance** for both fireplaces and wood stoves. Get your chimney cleaned regularly, and burn only properly seasoned dry wood. (Wet wood smokes.)

• **Buy a new wood stove** if yours was made before 1992, when stricter emission standards went into effect. Make sure it is sized properly for the area you wish to heat.

• **Limit candle burning**. (See "The Dark Side of Candles" on page 123.)

• **Check your kitchen exhaust fan** to be sure it is the right size and is vented to the outdoors. Use the fan every time you cook.

Many kitchen exhaust fans are so

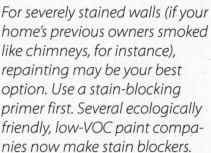

[smart tip]

Cover-Up

For severely stained walls (if your home's previous owners smoked like chimneys, for instance), repainting may be your best option. Use a stain-blocking primer first. Several ecologically friendly, low-VOC paint companies now make stain blockers.

powerful that they will pull air down the chimney (sucking soot and exhaust into your home) if they don't have any fresh air to bring inside. To avoid this, install a make-up air vent or open a window slightly while the fan is running.

Cleaning Dirty Walls

The method on page 115 is okay for most walls and ceilings that are painted, wood paneled, or vinyl wallpapered. But test-wash your wall in an inconspicuous area first, just to be sure. Use a large natural sponge (not a nylon one) found at janitorial supply centers, home centers, or hardware stores. Fill two buckets—one with the **All-Purpose Liquid Cleaner on page 39** and one with plain warm water. You may want to use an old sheet or blanket as a drop cloth to minimize mess on your floor.

• **Use an easy-to-clean finish** on the walls (at least below the chair rail) if you have small children. A low-VOC gloss or semigloss paint is a good option. Natural wood paneling also hides marks well. Avoid vinyl wallpaper. (It's easy to clean but made of toxic PVC.)

• **Buy water-soluble markers and paint.** (For a list of nontoxic art supplies, see watoxics.org.)

• **Keep art supplies** out of the hands of very young children except when they

A fireplace is a common source of dust, dirt, and soot. Installing tight-fitting glass doors can help.

DRY-CLEANING SPONGES

Rubber sponges, made from natural latex, can be used to clean everything from fireplaces to lamp shades.

When completely soiled, some brands can be washed. Allow them to dry completely before reuse.

can be supervised. Limit art projects to one particular area.

• **Hang chalkboards** or large sheets of paper on the wall so kids have a large surface upon which they may draw.

• **Get kids in the habit** of washing their hands whenever they get dirty. Provide a step stool for little ones and use a moisturizing soap so their

Cloth Wall Coverings

Natural fabrics are a nontoxic alternative to wallpaper. Vacuum cloth wall coverings with a soft brush attachment. Clean any stains with a method appropriate for the type of fabric.

hands feel good afterward.

• **Save the paint.** Whenever you paint a wall, save some of the paint. If there's a lot left, use the original container and tap the lid with a hammer to ensure a tight seal. If there's only a small amount left, pour it in a glass jar with a screw top. Label it with the paint brand, color number, and room you painted. When a wall is damaged, you'll always be able to do a quick touch-up.

Textured Ceilings

Ceilings that aren't smooth (such as those with "popcorn" texture or acoustic tiles) are a nightmare to clean. Your only choice really is to vacuum with a soft brush attachment. Don't get these types of ceilings wet because they may disintegrate. For small areas, try a rubber dry-cleaning sponge. (See page 116.)

Washing Walls

What you'll need: art gum eraser, dust mop, sponge, water, and two buckets

Vacuum or dust mop the entire wall. Then remove any obvious spots, marks, or stains from the wall. (See "Stain Removal" on page 116.) Using the **All-Purpose Liquid Cleaner on page 39,** begin washing at the bottom of the wall. Work your way up (to avoid drips drying on the wall before you reach them). Once you start washing a wall, keep up a steady pace and don't stop until you reach a corner—streaks will show if you overlap an area that has already dried. Keep your sponge clean by rinsing it frequently in a bucket of plain water, and replace the water in the bucket whenever it starts to look dirty.

Use a dust mop to wipe down the walls and remove dust and cobwebs.

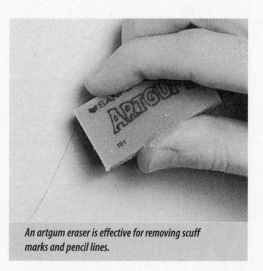

An artgum eraser is effective for removing scuff marks and pencil lines.

Start at the bottom and work your way up, being sure to keep your sponge clean.

An exhaust system that is properly sized for your range will not pull soot into your home.

Stain Removal

Walls are subject to everyday bumps and scuffs, even if you don't have kids. A lot of these scuff marks can be removed with an artgum eraser. It's a soft eraser that you can buy at office-supply or art-supply stores. It can be used even on delicate surfaces. Another tool is a rubber dry-cleaning sponge that is usually used for removing soot from walls and can be found at hardware stores. Rubbing dry baking soda or cornstarch onto a spot with a clean cloth can also be effective. If these options don't work, try the following stain-specific remedies. (Always test in an inconspicuous spot first!)

Crayons: Rub with a plain white (non-gel) toothpaste. Then rub with a paste of washing soda and water. (Wear gloves—washing soda can irritate skin.)

Markers: Alcohol is often your best bet for ink and marker stains. I don't recommend rubbing alcohol because it is highly toxic when ingested. Vodka is a better option. Don't rub ink stains. Just continue to blot them gently with a clean cloth. Refold the cloth frequently so that you are always using a clean section.

Cooking grease: Wipe it down with a rag or sponge that's been dipped in warm water and a squirt of hand dishwashing liquid.

Fingerprints and body oil: Areas on and around light switches, door knobs, and hand rails often get coated with oil and grime from dirty hands. Spray the area with full-strength vinegar, and wipe clean.

If you want to reduce the use of environmentally harmful finishes, lower VOC levels, and make cleaning easier, install unpainted wood paneling on walls and ceilings.

Prefinished ceilings, such as this tin pattern, eliminate the need to paint and can withstand scrubbing better than painted ceilings.

Whether it's a stair railing or a favorite vase or a bathtub faucet, the home is filled with metal objects. Acids, such as vinegar, lemon juice, or tomato juice, usually clean them best, and sometimes an abrasive, such as salt, is added to provide more scrubbing power.

Aluminum: Put the aluminum item in a large pot; fill the pot with water; and add three lemons (or one grapefruit) that have been cut in half. Simmer on low for several hours; then polish the item with a clean rag. Or make a paste of cream of tartar and vinegar. Rub the paste on the stain and let it dry completely before rinsing. *Do not use baking soda or washing soda on aluminum.*

Brass: Make a paste of lemon juice and table salt. Rub it on the stain until clean, then rinse and dry.

Chrome: Spray on club soda and polish chrome with a soft cloth until dry. Rub rust spots with aluminum foil or fine steel wool. Protect chrome with a coat of wax.

Copper: Rub copper with ketchup or tomato paste; let it sit for an hour or so; and then rinse and dry. Or carefully dip it in boiling vinegar, rinse with water, and wipe dry.

Gold: Use a plain white, non-gel toothpaste and a soft brush on gold. Rinse with water, and dry.

Iron: Dip a cloth or sponge in olive oil and rub rust spots until they are gone.

Stainless steel: To remove water spots, spray with club soda or vinegar and polish with a soft cloth. You can use fresh lemon juice to remove rust stains, but you must let it sit for several hours.

Green Fact

According to the book *Why Your House May Endanger Your Health* by Alfred V. Zamm, MD, the average six-room house accumulates about 40 pounds of dust per year. Household dust can contain hair, pet dander, skin flakes, textile fibers, paint particles, and more.

A little club soda keeps chrome bath fixtures shining like new.

Microfiber cloths have really revolution-ized dusting—at least for me! Their thousands of tiny fibers pick up dust and trap it with ease. I'm referring to the cloths you can wash and reuse hun-dreds of times. Avoid the throwaway kind. It is more environmentally friendly to reuse items than to discard them. Just vacuum your microfiber dust cloth and launder it whenever needed. (Don't wash it with lint-producing fabrics because the microfiber picks up all the lint.) A drawback is that microfiber cloth is petroleum-based, which isn't great for the environment. For a more natural option, try a lambs-wool duster instead.

When you vacuum your floors, use the hose and soft-brush attachment to remove dust from baseboard moldings, shelves, the tops of furniture, uphol-stery, window treatments, and electron-ic equipment. Take care around elec-tronics because many of them are treat-ed with PDBEs (toxic flame retardants) that contaminate the dust around them. Use a vacuum with HEPA filtra-tion to isolate the PDBEs and prevent them from recirculating in your home.

The vacuum is a quick and easy way to dust books and shelves.

THE DARK SIDE OF CANDLES

In the last few years, home inspectors and insurance adjusters have seen a dramatic increase in the number of homes reporting soot-stained walls. One of the causes? Scented candles. In today's airtight, energy-efficient homes, what burns in the home stays in the home. One tester burned four candles for 15 hours straight in a home and had to stop the test for fear of doing "too much damage"—already soot was visible on the walls, curtains, dishwasher, refrigerator, and air-conditioner filter. Some apartment buildings have instituted a "no open flame" policy to combat this problem.

In addition to unsightly soot, candles can also be a health hazard. Most scented candles are made from paraffin wax (a petroleum product), and many of the fragrances are synthetic hydrocarbons. One study that tested soot particles from 30 randomly selected candles found traces of benzene, acetone, styrene, lead, and other toxins.

Your safest option is to avoid using candles (or anything else that burns, such as incense or oil lamps) inside your home—burn them outside on your deck or patio instead.

One alternative is an essential oil diffuser, such as a lamp ring or clay pot diffuser.

If you can't resist the ambiance scented candles provide, use the following guidelines to minimize risk:

❑ Try 100-percent beeswax or soy candles—they burn cleaner and produce less black soot.

❑ Look for products that use only natural essential oils for fragrance.

❑ Keep candle wicks trimmed to ¼ inch at all times and keep them out of drafts—a low, steady-burning flame produces the least amount of soot.

❑ Long-burning candles tend to flicker more. Instead, use two identical candles—burn one for an hour, and then extinguish it and light the other one.

❑ Avoid jar candles that have a narrow mouth, which can restrict airflow and make flames flicker.

❑ Avoid wicks with metal in them—wicks should be made from natural plant fiber and curl as they burn.

❑ Synthetic carpet fibers collect soot particles. Vacuum carpets and rugs frequently using a vacuum with a HEPA filter. (Regular vacuum cleaners will just spread the soot.)

❑ Use a high-efficiency filter on your forced hot-air or air-conditioning system, and replace it regularly.

❑ Open your windows and doors to let in fresh air frequently.

When cleaning a mirror, apply club soda to your cloth. Do not spray the mirror directly.

Mirrors and Tabletops

I find a spray bottle of club soda works best for small inside jobs. A non-toxic store-bought glass cleaner will work fine, too. Spray the solution on a sponge or cloth, wash down the glass, and then wipe with a separate clean, dry cloth. (Microfiber cloths work well to remove any spots.) Don't spray solution directly onto a mirror because moisture can get behind the glass and damage the silvering, causing unsightly dark spots.

"Essential oils make homemade recipes so much more enjoyable. I love how I can customize the scent to suit my mood. My favorites are lemon, cedarwood, and eucalyptus." – J.S.

AIR PURIFIERS

When it comes to clean air, the best option is to remove any causes of indoor air pollution from your home, and to live someplace where the outdoor air is clean. But there are plenty of cases where this isn't possible, and you may want to consider some type of air filtration device.

Air purifiers can be built into your central-heating and air-conditioning system, or you can purchase a portable room model. There are many types of purifiers, and you will have to focus on what type of pollutants you wish to filter out in order to pick the best device for your needs.

Consider the following when researching purifiers:

❑ Whether you need to filter chemicals (from materials off-gassing in your home or from sources outside your home) or particulate matter (pollen, animal dander, mold, and so forth) or both.

❑ The size of the area from which you want to remove pollutants. Portable air filters come in several sizes depending on the square footage you wish to clean. Cubic footage is a better gauge than square footage—if your ceilings are higher than the average 8 feet, take that into account.

❑ Determine which parts, such as filters, will need maintenance—how much will they cost, and how often will they need to be replaced so you can calculate the annual cost of running it.

❑ What type of maintenance is required.

❑ How much noise an air purifier makes—especially if you're going to have it in your bedroom.

All About Floors

Throughout the book, there are a few basic housekeeping principles that I stress repeatedly. These principles are particularly important when discussing flooring.

The first is prevention. You'll have to clean a lot less if you prevent dirt from getting into your home in the first place. I added large mats inside and outside of all my exterior doors and was amazed at the difference it made.

The second is upkeep. Light cleaning regularly is a lot easier and takes less time in the end than heavy cleaning occasionally. Regular cleaning is also the key to preserving your floor's finish and maintaining its overall appearance.

The third principle is smart material selection. When buying new flooring, I always consider how easy it will be to clean, and how it affects indoor air quality.

The split tips on the bristles of a nylon broom, left, sweep up particles better than natural fibers. An easy way to clean up spills is to use your dust pan and squeegee.

"Sometimes green cleaning just means being resourceful and finding other ways to do things."

Nothing in the home gets more wear and tear than floors—and tracking dirt indoors on your shoes doesn't help. As with most other areas of the home, the first line of green defense is prevention. Not only does dirt look bad, but its abrasiveness means it causes a lot of damage to your floor's finish. In addition, you can also drag in toxins, such as pesticides, that have accumulated in the dust outside your doors.

Here are some tips to keep out the dirt:

• **Make it a house policy to take off your shoes** when you come in the door. Leave adequate space by each door to store shoes. (If you are short on space, tiered shoe racks are available.) Buy your kids shoes that are easy for them to put on and take off quickly.

• **Use mats at every entrance** (including the garage). Cleaning guru Don Aslett recommends a 5-foot-long mat both inside and outside each door. Buy high-quality commercial-grade mats made of nylon or polypropylene with a rubber (not vinyl) backing.

• **Teach dogs to stop at the door** so you can wipe off their feet when they're muddy. Keep a rag near the door for this purpose.

Floor Tools

Investing in high-quality cleaning tools makes a lot of sense—they clean better and faster and last longer, which is good for you and the environment. A janitorial-supply center (either a brick-and-mortar or an Internet store) is your best source for these items. Some home-improvement stores and warehouse membership clubs sell janitorial supplies, too.

Consider the following floor-care arsenal:

Broom: Look for an angled broom with soft nylon bristles.

Dust pan: Look for a large, heavy-duty pan made of hard plastic or metal. One with high sides is better because you can use it with a squeegee to clean up spills.

Microfiber mop: I like to use a microfiber mop for dust, damp, and wet

Steam is a great way to clean and disinfect floors without the use of harsh cleansers.

mopping. You can buy different-size microfiber pads for each type of job; they are machine washable, so you can use them repeatedly. Look for a mop that has a wide swivel head (15 to 18 inches) and a long handle that comes up to your shoulder.

Rubber broom: This unique tool has rubber bristles on one side and a squeegee on the other. It is great for sweeping, removing pet hair, and clean-ing up spills. It can even be used as a mop. (See "Tile, Stone, Rubber, Vinyl, and Concrete," on page 134.) Always pull the rubber broom toward you—don't push. (I always tease my mom for buying "mir-acle" products at the fair every year, but this one really is great!)

Vacuum: See page 50 for the full scoop on choosing a vacuum.

Steam cleaner: See page 49 for more information on steam cleaners.

When buying flooring, consider how easy it will be to clean and maintain. Bamboo, shown here, is cleaned like wood. A type of grass, it is a fast-growing, renewable resource. See page 132 for care suggestions.

These types of flooring can be damaged by excessive water, so avoid wet mopping. The key is to remove the dirt before it gets ground in, by dust mopping, sweeping, or vacuuming frequently. High-traffic areas should be cleaned several times a week. Vacuums are heavy and noisy, and they consume electricity, so sweeping or dust mopping is usually a better option. If you do vacuum, use an attachment that has soft bristles or felt on the bottom so it doesn't scratch. (Don't use a vacuum with the beater bar turned on because it can damage hard floors.)

Dust Mopping

Dust mopping with a microfiber mop (with a dust pad attached) is quick and easy. I find it faster than sweeping, and it picks up finer particles. The microfiber attracts dust while completely dry—no cleaning solution is needed. Just run it along your floor using an S-shaped motion—not only does it pick up dust, but it will push along any other crumbs

LOWDOWN ON LINOLEUM

True linoleum (not to be confused with vinyl) is a great, environmentally friendly flooring choice. It is made out of linseed oil, tree resins, powdered wood or cork, limestone, and pigments. With proper care it can last up to 40 years, and it is completely recyclable. When cleaning it, avoid alkaline products such as baking soda, borax, or washing soda. Use a mild soap or vinegar instead. Linoleum requires occasional sealing, and there are nontoxic sealers available—check with a green-building supply store.

Damp Mopping

Microfiber pads attach easily to the mop. Shown here is a dust-mop pad (bottom) and a wet/dry pad (top).

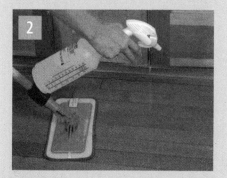

Wood floors can be damaged or discolored by large amounts of water, so a light misting with a spray bottle works well.

A gentle scrubbing with a mop easily removes grime. Be sure to clean your mop pad frequently so you don't spread the dirt.

it encounters. Leave the crumbs in a pile and finish up with a dust pan. Vacuum the dust pad to clean it and throw it in the wash occasionally with other cleaning rags. Most companies claim their pads can withstand hundreds of washings.

Damp Mopping

When you need more serious cleaning, try damp mopping. Again, a microfiber mop (above) works great, but a sponge mop could also be used. Dust mop or sweep before you start. Use either the **All-Purpose Liquid Cleaner on page 39** or the **Glass Cleaner on page 40.** (Vinegar is fine for light cleaning; use the all-purpose cleaner for more serious grime removal.) Otherwise, you can use your favorite store-bought nontoxic floor cleaner.

Wet your mop pad with water, and

then wring it out as thoroughly as possible. Using a spray bottle, *very* lightly spray a 4 x 6-foot area of the floor. Let the solution sit on the floor for 20 seconds or so, and then gently scrub it with your microfiber mop. Continue on to the next spot, spraying then mopping. When your mop pad gets dirty, rinse it out in the sink and keep going. Wash it in the washing machine when you're done. This method can also be used on carpets. (See page 138.)

TILE, STONE, RUBBER, VINYL, AND CONCRETE

These surfaces should be cared for the same way as indicated in the earlier section on hardwood floors. Sweeping is still your first line of defense. Tile and stone can be tricky because uneven surfaces are prone to collecting dirt. I

Acid-etched concrete floors are inexpensive, environmentally sound, tough, beautiful, and easy to keep clean.

like the rubber broom best in these cases—it manages to sweep up the dirt instead of just pushing it into the grout lines and crevices. Vacuums with a soft-brush attachment also work well in these situations.

Wet Mopping

Tile, stone, rubber, and vinyl are fairly impervious to water, so you can use the old mop and bucket routine. If your floor is laden with grime, try the wet-mopping method that I discovered in *Organic Housekeeping* by Ellen Sandbeck. (See below.)

[smart tip]

Seal It

If you have unsealed concrete, stone, or cork flooring, consider sealing it. There are eco-friendly sealers available, and they will make cleaning a whole lot easier.

Wet Mopping Floors

What you'll need: rubber broom, rags, and a bucket

*Grab about a dozen clean rags and a rubber broom. (A push broom or a sponge mop would also work.) Drop a rag in a bucket of the **All-Purpose Liquid Cleaner on page 39;** spread it on the floor; and scrub the rag against the floor with the rubber broom or mop. Keep moving the rag until it gets too dry. Then set it aside, grab a new rag, and repeat the process. When the solution and rags are always clean, you never have to deal with a dirty mop or dirty water! Launder the rags when you're done.*

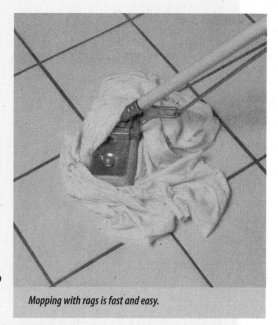

Mopping with rags is fast and easy.

Soapstone resists acids and staining. It does not need to be sealed, and scratches can be sanded away.

Carpets and rugs require frequent cleaning. If you don't pick up dirt quickly, it gets ground into the carpet, where it looks bad and damages the carpet fibers. Depending on the number of people and pets in your home and how dirty their feet are, you should probably vacuum high-traffic areas several times a week. The good news is, a quick vacuuming is all that carpets really need to stay looking good for years.

Carpet Sweepers

Vacuuming is a chore I dislike more than almost any other—I can't stand the noise. I do have rugs in my home, though, so I used to drag the vacuum out all the time. Then I remembered my grandmother. She used to follow us around with her carpet sweeper. If you haven't seen one, it's sort of a cross between a broom and a vacuum. It

Surface Cleaning

Damp mopping your carpets once a month can help keep them looking good and prolong the amount of time between deep cleans. The idea is to remove the surface grime and stains. You can use the same damp mop method used for hard flooring shown on page 133. Use one part vinegar and one part water in a spray bottle. (Don't use any soap or detergent because it will leave a residue that needs rinsing.) Be sure to spray very lightly—you just want to clean the surface, and the carpet should be dry again minutes after you mop it.

uses no electricity, which means no noise and no cord to get tangled. I love it! It takes care of everyday dirt, doesn't wake up sleeping children, and means I only have to drag out the vacuum once a week. It also works well on hard floors.

Deep Cleaning

You should probably deep clean your carpets every 2 to 5 years, depending on the number of people and pets in your family, the

[smart tip]

Kids and Floors

It's especially important to have a nontoxic floor if you have kids. They spend most of their time playing on the floor, and because they are lower to the ground they are more likely to breathe in dust and chemicals present in the flooring.

A carpet sweeper is an effective way to quickly clean up crumbs without hauling out a vacuum.

"Don't buy a cheap vacuum. It will do a poor job and won't last. If you can't afford the top of the line, buy a good used machine that's been refurbished. Vacuums designed for commercial use will rarely wear out with home use, so they are a good bet." – J.S.

amount of dirt that gets tracked, and how frequently you vacuum. Do it *before* the carpets start to get really grungy and sticky. You can rent a carpet-cleaning machine and do the job yourself, or hire a service.

If you do it yourself, use a nontoxic product specially formulated for carpets. Use the minimum amount of shampoo directed and pay special attention to the rinse/extraction instructions. The reason it is said that "carpets get dirtier faster after being cleaned" is because improper cleaning leaves

Green Fact

Bamboo was introduced as flooring in the early 1990s and has captured a significant share of the market with its clean Asian look. It is a popular eco flooring choice because, as a grass, it is a rapidly renewable resource that can be harvested every 3 to 6 years.

Loop-pile carpets, such as Berber (above), cable, and multilevel loop styles, hold up well to traffic, hide footprints, and are easier to clean than cut-pile carpets.

Loop Pile

Cut and Loop

[smart **tip**]

Odor Eater

To remove odors from rugs or carpets, sprinkle baking soda on the rug and work it in gently with a broom. Let it sit overnight, and then vacuum.

detergent residue in the carpet that becomes a magnet for dirt.

If you have a professional service clean your carpets, look for one that uses the truck-mounted hot-water extraction method. It is the most powerful and can pull the most dirt out of your carpet. You may be able to find one that uses an environmentally friendly carpet shampoo. (See Resources on page 218.) You could also ask if you could supply the shampoo or if they could clean with just hot water. Refuse any type of protective, stain-fighting treatment. Always check references before hiring.

Carpet-Stain Removal

When treating a stain, remember to wet the carpet as little as possible because it is difficult to dry it afterward. A wet/dry vacuum is really helpful in these situations to suck up excess moisture. (Note: wool carpets can be particularly tricky, so double-check with your dealer before following these instructions.) For most stains, you can follow the general method on page 145.

Area rugs are better than wall-to-wall carpets because they can be carried outside for cleaning.

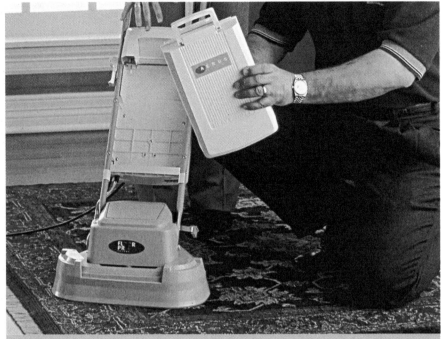

If you're using a carpet-cleaning machine, choose eco-friendly cleaners that leave no residue behind.

Snow Cleaning

You'd think that, being from snowy northern Vermont, I would have heard of this method for cleaning rugs, but I actually just read about it recently. I haven't tried it yet, but according to reports, it cleans and restores vibrant colors. (Note: if you have an expensive rug, you should check with a professional to make sure this method is safe for it.) Pick a cold day (25 degrees F or lower) when you have plenty of dry, powdery snow on the ground, not the packing kind good for making snowballs. First, put your rug outside for several hours to bring it down to the outside temperature (so that it does not melt the snow). Then lay it out in the snow facedown. Now gently walk on it or beat it with a broom. Massage the fibers, don't mash them. When the snow underneath gets dirty, move to a new spot. Keep moving until the snow underneath stays clean. When done, gently brush or shake the snow off the rug and bring it back inside.

Removing Carpet Stains

What you'll need: white towel or rag, dustpan, club soda, dish soap, small container, water, egg beater or whisk, brush or sponge, and a fan

Take action as soon as possible. First, use a clean white towel or rag to blot up as much moisture as you can. Don't scrub because that could spread the stain. Always work from the outside of the stain inward. Scrape off any solids into a dustpan. Next, spray club soda on the stain, wait

1

Blot the stain, in this case ketchup, with a clean towel or rag. Do not scrub.

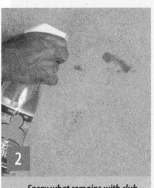

2

Spray what remains with club soda and wait 30 seconds before blotting again.

30 seconds, and blot. Repeat several times until the stain stops coming off on the towel. Once the stain is gone, dry the area as described below.

If the stain persists, try dish soap. Put a table-spoon of dish soap in a small container and add ½ cup cold water. Using an egg beater or whisk, whip the solution until it is foam. Gently apply the foam to the spot, pressing it down into the stain with a brush or sponge. Wait 30 seconds, and then blot. Repeat several times. After apply-ing dish soap, you will need to rinse; otherwise the soap residue will attract dirt. Put a small amount of water on a clean sponge and wet the spot, and then blot dry. Repeat several times.

Finally, dry the spot as thoroughly as you can because a damp carpet can mildew or rot. Use a wet/dry vac if you have one. If the spot is still damp, set up a fan and leave it blowing on the spot overnight.

3

Use a fan to dry carpeting after removing the stain.

Caring for Furnishings

Furnishings get a lot of wear and tear in my home—especially because I have children and pets. Keeping my furnishings in good shape means that they'll last longer. This helps the environment because I'll contribute less to landfills and have to buy fewer new items.

A lot of commercial furniture-care products, such as polishes and waxes, contain chemicals that irritate your lungs and skin. Many are labeled "harmful or fatal if swallowed," which should always give you pause.

This chapter covers healthier methods for cleaning everything from dining tables and sofas to computers and blinds.

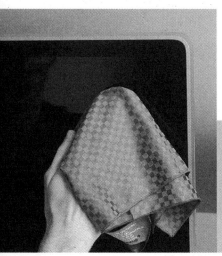

Microfiber cloths, left, are excellent for dusting everything from electronics, such as this computer screen, to woodwork. They can be used wet or dry. For your upholstery, stick with natural fabrics, such as cotton, right.

"Many green cleaning techniques were ones used by your great-grandparents and continue to make sense today."

Conventional furniture polishes are bad for a lot of reasons. They often contain toxic ingredients. Even plain "lemon oil" is really mineral oil (a petroleum product) and artificial dye and fragrance—no lemons at all! Many polishes still use aerosol propellants, which are respiratory irritants and contribute to smog. And those with silicone leave a film that is difficult to remove, making future repairs or restoration to the wood challenging. But I have to confess, I love the way furniture polish smells and the wood shines after I polish it. So are there alternatives? Yes.

Wood Cleaning

Most of the time, dusting is all you really need to do to care for wood furniture. No special dusting spray is needed—just use a dry microfiber cloth or a lambs-wool duster. A few drops of lemon essential oil on your cloth will give provide the lemony scent that you may miss.

If wood needs more than dusting, make sure it can withstand cleaning. Check to see if the finish is cracked, peeling, or worn. If it is damaged, you may have to strip and refinish the piece or, especially if it's an antique, have it

Wood Care

As is the case with so many things, an ounce of prevention is worth a pound of cure. Here are some guidelines for taking care of your valuable wood furniture:

• **Keep wood out of direct sunlight** whenever possible because light can cause bleaching and discoloration. Use blinds or curtains to block the sun, or use an opaque tablecloth on tables.

• **Try to avoid** extreme swings in the relative humidity in your home. Wood expands as the moisture in the air rises, and contracts as the air gets drier. This movement can warp and split the wood and cause finishes to crack and peel.

• **Avoid placing wood furniture** near sources of heat, such as stoves, fireplaces, or heating vents.

• **Use coasters,** trivets, tablecloths, and ink blotters to protect wood surfaces.

• **Put felt pads** on the bottom of lamps, vases, and so forth to prevent them from scratching.

• **Clean spills** immediately—the longer they sit, the greater chance they have of sinking through the finish and into the wood itself.

Wood furniture can last for generations—and it doesn't off-gas chemicals that pollute the indoor air.

"My dining room set has been in my family for many genera-tions, and I'd like to think my great-grandmother cared for the table the same way that I do." – J.S.

PROTECTING WITH WAX

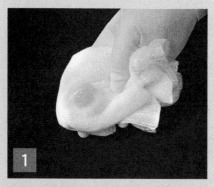

1

Saturate an applicator, such as a cheesecloth, with wax and wipe with circular strokes.

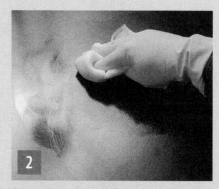

2

Once you've applied a thin film over the surface, allow it to stand for 20 minutes or as recommended.

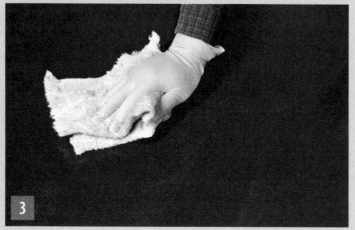

3

Finish by buffing with a clean cloth. Turn the cloth frequently as you go, and be sure to wipe up any excess wax. Opt for waxes made without petroleum-based solvents whenever possible.

evaluated by a professional furniture restorer.

If the finish is in good shape, try cleaning with soap and water. Never apply the water directly to the wood surface. Instead, wet the cloth; wring it out completely; and then wipe the surface. Once the surface is clean, dry it immediately with a soft cloth. If soap and water don't do the trick, you may have to resort to a solvent. A citrus-based solvent is least toxic, but use it with good ventilation.

Spots, Scratches, and More

Try the following remedies for common problems:

White haze and glass rings: White haze and rings are caused by moisture that gets into the finish and does not evaporate. Rub any type of oil (such as olive oil or coconut oil) into the ring, and let it sit until the whiteness disappears; then wipe it off with a dry cloth.

Scratches: Find a crayon similar in color to your wood. (Woodworking stores carry special "filler sticks" for this purpose.) Apply the crayon to the scratch, and heat the area gently with a hair dryer to soften the crayon wax. Keep applying the crayon until the scratch is filled, and then buff it with a soft, dry cloth. If the surface is waxed, apply wax to the repaired area and buff.

Stickers: To remove stickers or paper that's stuck to a wood, metal, or glass surface, apply repeated coats of any oil (such as olive oil), saturating the area. Then gently rub it with a soft cloth until the you loosen the paper. You can also use a nontoxic citrus-based adhesive remover.

Green Fact

Phenol, a toxic crystalline acidic compound found in some pine disinfectants and furniture polishes, is so deadly that it was used by the Nazis to execute prisoners during World War II. Phenol injections were given to thousands of people in concentration camps.

Wax or Polish?

A semisolid paste wax, rather than a spray or liquid polish, is the best way to protect your furniture. It provides a protective coating to any finish—oil, varnish, shellac, lacquer, polyurethane, or paint—and it can be buffed to a high shine. It's difficult to find a paste wax without petroleum-based ingredients or solvents, but there are some. (See Resources.)

Annie Berthold-Bond offers several recipes for making your own wax in her book *Better Basics for the Home*. Be sure to read the technique for proper waxing because it takes practice.

Apply wax only to finishes that are in good condition. Wax areas that show heavy wear, such as desktops, chair arms, every six months. Wax chair legs, the sides of cabinets, and other slow-wearing areas only every three or four years.

[smart tip]

Acids and Drying Oils

Avoid combining acids, such as vinegar or lemon juice, with "drying oils" —linseed, flax, walnut, or tung oil. A chemical reaction with acid causes these oils to turn a dark muddy brown or black. Unfortunately, many traditional recipes combine these ingredients (usually linseed oil and vinegar), which is why so many antiques are dark in color.

Solid wood is actually a rarity in today's furniture market. Most furniture sold in the United States has veneers or laminate finishes. You must take greater care with these pieces because the finishes can be damaged easily and are sometimes difficult to repair.

Metal and glass are also popular choices today. For cleaning metal, refer to page 120.

Glass Tabletops

I find that a spritz of club soda from a spray bottle works best. A nontoxic store-bought glass cleaner will do fine too. (See Resources.) Spray the solution on a sponge or cloth; wipe the glass; and then go over the surface with a clean, dry cloth. (Microfiber cloths work well to remove spots.) To remove scratches, try rubbing them with plain white toothpaste, and then polish the surface with a soft cloth.

Veneers and Laminates

Furniture that's made of fiberboard, such as particleboard, medium-density fiberboard (MDF), and high-density fiberboard, is cheaper than solid wood. These materials are composed of wood fibers or chips that are bound with a resin and pressed into panels under high heat. The panels aren't pretty, but they are finished with a thin, real-wood or plastic-laminate veneer.

Basic caring for these veneers is pretty much the same as that for solid wood. Keep the furniture dusted, and clean with soap and water when it's needed. Use water conservatively near the seams (where one piece of veneer or laminate meets another); moisture can cause the edges to curl.

Even plastic laminates can be waxed—it will provide an extra layer of protection from scratches and stains in high-use areas, and it can revive spots where the shiny finish has become dull or worn.

Stains and scratches on real-wood veneers can be treated the same as those on solid wood. Be careful not to destroy the veneer if you sand.

Stains on plastic-laminate veneers can be treated like those on countertops made of the same material. (See page 76.) However, scratches are almost impossible to fix, so you may need to find a way to cover them.

[smart **tip**]

Finish the Unfinished

Unfinished wood is extremely difficult to keep clean and is vulnerable to stains caused by moisture. It is also susceptible to fading due to sun exposure. Consider finishing it with a nontoxic oil, wax, or sealer, or painting it with a low-VOC paint.

Wicker Furniture

Vacuum wicker with the soft-brush attachment. Use a dry paintbrush to get dust out of nooks and crannies, and a damp cloth dipped in mild soap and water to remove grime. Wipe it with a dry cloth, leaving it in the sun to eliminate any remaining moisture. Scrub synthetic wicker with a mild biodegradable detergent, and rinse with a hose.

Tile and Stone Tabletops

For cleaning tile, marble, granite, slate, and other stone, follow the basic advice supplied for veneers and laminates on page 153. Dust these surfaces frequently, and wash them with mild soap and water. Some other tips:

Tile: Use vinegar or other acids as infrequently as possible—both the tile and grout can be etched by acid. To clean grout, try the **Baking Soda Scrub on page 44.** Be sure to rinse immediately with water after using vinegar. A new stiff-bristle toothbrush will help you scrub. You may want to consider sealing the grout with a nontoxic sealant to keep it clean. (See Resources.)

Marble: Vinegar and other acids will ruin marble, so avoid using them. For stains, try a paste of baking soda and water. Apply the paste to the stain; let it sit for 15 minutes; then rinse it with water and wipe it with a dry cloth. Seal marble with a nontoxic sealer yearly.

Granite: Sprinkle greasy stains with a liberal amount of cornstarch; let it sit for about 10 minutes; and then it rinse with soap and water.

Slate: Grease can stain slate as well. Remove it by using the same method decribed above for granite. Seal slate surfaces with a nontoxic sealer yearly.

Use cornstarch to lift oily stains from granite.

UPHOLSTERY

Upholstered furniture has some type of padding covered by fabric or leather. When you're cleaning upholstery, it's important to keep the padding dry. If the padding gets wet, it is prone to mold and deterioration. Here are some general tips for caring for upholstery.

• **Protect upholstered furniture** from the effects of harsh sunlight by using blinds or coated window treatments..

• **Avoid high humidity levels,** which can encourage the growth of mildew.

• **Use covers** on the arms of chairs to protect them from soil and wear.

Cleaning Upholstery

What you'll need: sponge, cloth, water, and vinegar

For light soil, try a solution of one part water and one part vinegar. Vinegar won't get out heavy grime or stains, but it's a good cleaner for light soils—and you don't have to rinse it afterward. Apply a small amount of the solution to the fabric, using a slightly damp sponge or cloth, or give it a light spritz from a spray bottle. Rub gently; let it sit for a minute; and then pat the spot with a dry cloth to absorb any moisture.

Cleaning Stubborn Stains

What you'll need: dish soap, small container, water, egg beater or whisk, cloth, sponge, and a fan

For heavier soils or stains, use dish soap and water. Put a tablespoon of the soap in a small container and add ½ cup cold water. Using an egg beater or whisk, whip the solution until it's foamy. Apply the foam to the fabric;

Apply soap foam to the stain with a spoon or bowl scraper. Rub with a sponge, and then rinse.

Beat water and dish soap to make a stain remover for fabric.

rub gently with a dry cloth or sponge; let it sit for a minute; and then rinse. (If you don't rinse the spot, the soap residue will attract more dirt.) Put a small amount of water on a clean sponge and wet the fabric (or lightly mist it with a spray bottle), and then wipe off as much moisture as you can with a dry cloth. Rinse several times. If the fabric still feels damp, try this: set up a fan and let it blow on the area overnight. This will speed up the drying process and prevent mold.

Cleaning Leather

Leather is a great low-maintenance covering for furniture, but it can get dry and crack. That's a good reason for not using solvents or alcohol to clean leather. Dust leather regularly to keep ground dirt from getting under the top surface.

The best choice to both clean and moisturize leather is liquid saddle soap. It is used to maintain horse saddles and bridles, and it can be found at a local tack shop. You can also buy it online.

Use the saddle soap undiluted—you don't need any water to apply it, and you don't rinse it. Put a small amount on a clean, dry cloth. Using a circular motion, rub the soap into the leather. Let it sit for a minute, and then buff the surface with another dry cloth. On a large piece of furniture, work one section at a time. It's important to keep the soap from sitting on the leather too long before you buff it.

Saddle soap is also great for cleaning leather upholstery and surfaces.

Stained Upholstery Guidelines

1. Quick action is essential for upholstery stains—the deeper the stain sinks into the fabric and padding, the more difficult it is to remove.

2. Never rub a fresh stain—gently blot it with a white cloth or paper towel, working from the outside toward the center of the stain. Cautiously scrape off any solids with a spatula or spoon without damaging the fabric.

3. Rinse protein stains (egg, milk, urine, blood, and so forth) with cold water or club soda. (Always make sure your cleaning solution is cold because warm or hot water can "cook" the protein and make the stain permanent.)

4. Pretreat oil-based stains (cooking oil, food grease, motor oil, and so forth) by applying hand-dishwashing soap foam directly to the stain and blotting it gently. (See page 156.)

5. Blot tannin stains (red wine, coffee, tea, juice, ketchup, soft drinks, and so forth) with club soda. If that doesn't work, try dishwasher detergent. (See page 156.) The oils in soap can set these stains, so detergent is more effective in this instance.

6. After treating any stain, use the rinsing and drying method that is described on page 156.

[smart tip]

Choose Natural

When buying upholstered furniture, choose natural fabrics, such as ramie or wool, and padding, such as cotton or goose down. Avoid polyurethane foam and flame-retardant coatings.

Cleaning Fabric

As mentioned on page 155, you should not get upholstery very wet. Once water soaks into the padding it's hard to dry it. For basic maintenance, regular cleaning should be done using a vacuum with a soft-brush attachment. The more frequently you vacuum, the less chance soil has to get ground into fibers. When vacuuming isn't enough, try the cleaning methods on page 156. (Test them in an inconspicuous spot first—some delicate fabrics are dry clean only.)

It's easy to ignore window treatments— after a while you may barely notice them because they become so much a part of a room you see every day. But regular care will help them last longer. In addition, fabric can become a haven for dust mites and other allergens, so if anyone suffers from allergies in your family, you will need to wash fabric treatments regularly—or use hard treatments instead. See the following pages for tips on cleaning common window treatments, including curtains, shades, shutters, and blinds.

RESIST STAIN-RESISTANT

Low levels of perfluorooctanoic acid (PFOA), an integral chemical used to produce stain-resistant treatments in everything from pans to textiles, has been found in the environment and in the blood of the general population of the United States. Some studies have raised concerns about the health effects this exposure may cause.

At this time, the Environmental Protection Agency (EPA) has not made a recommendation to stop consumers from using products containing PFOA because its effects are not fully understood. However, manufacturers who use PFOA have agreed to phase it out by 2015.

I recommend avoiding home furnishings treated with this chemical until more information becomes available. Stain-resistant upholstery, carpets, and floors may be convenient, but the safest remedy for stains and soiling remains is diligent care. Clean stains immediately, vacuum often, and deep-clean furnishings as needed.

The green choice for carpeting is a natural fiber, including wool, silk, seagrass, sisal, jute, and combinations of them.

Shutters

Shutters can be vacuumed with a soft-brush attachment. If there is built-up dust and grime, and the shutters need a thorough cleaning, remove them from their hinges, and lay them flat on a table with a towel underneath. If you have plastic shutters, you can spray them with a solution of hand-dishwashing soap and water or with your favorite all-purpose, nontoxic cleaner.

Scrub nooks and crannies with a toothbrush, rinse with water, and then dry them thoroughly. If you have wood shutters, don't get them too wet. Instead, wipe them with a damp sponge dipped in a solution of hand-dishwashing soap and water. Rinse with a damp sponge, and then wipe with a clean, dry cloth. Dry nooks and crannies with a cloth wrapped around the end of a butter knife or screwdriver.

Curtains

Vacuum curtains regularly with a soft-brush attachment to keep dust from accumulating. If they can be easily removed, take them outside and give them a good shaking and let them air in the sun for an hour or two. If they can be washed, launder them once or twice a year (more frequently if a family member has allergies). Be sure to use cold water and a delicate wash cycle, and air-dry them afterward to prevent shrinking or damage to the fabric. Be sure to note where any folds or creases are in case you need to iron curtains to smooth out wrinkles.

Blinds

Lower horizontal blinds (or extend vertical blinds) all the way, and then adjust them so they are fully closed. Vacuum them with a soft brush attachment. Then vacuum the other side by adjusting the controls until the blinds rotate completely in the other direction and lay flat.

If the blinds are grimey, take them outside, hose them, and wipe both sides with a warm, soapy rag. Let them dry in the sun, and then bring them back inside. (If the blinds are wood, don't soak them—you will have to wipe them with a damp rag instead.)

Shades

Fabric shades are generally delicate, often laminated to vinyl, and have hardware attached—so they're hard to wash. You can vacuum all types of shades with a soft-brush attachment. Use a damp sponge to wipe down vinyl shades and to spot treat fabric shades. To dry, open the window and pull down the shade completely .

Wood blinds should be cleaned with a soft-brush vacuum attachment. For built-up grime, use a rag or sponge dampened with a mild detergent. To avoid warping, do not soak wood.

DIRTY JOBS Part III

Outside the House

I enjoy outdoor cleaning projects. They're a nice excuse to spend time outside on a pleasant day. Save these projects for the warm, sunny days of summer. Working with a hose or pressure washer in the cold is a lot less fun.

Cleaning a house exterior requires a little fore-thought, but it shouldn't give anyone a headache. There are many simple tasks that you can do on your own, and there's no shortage of helpful, ecologically friendly products and services out there.

That's important because cleaning the exterior of a house isn't only about sprucing. It 's also about removing the dirt and grime that, over time, can cause structural damage. Cleaning also exposes any immediate flaws—mold, rot, and rust—that need to be addressed. Many of the same techniques can be used on decks, patios, and outdoor furniture.

Household-size pressure washers, left, are capable cleaners for many outdoor jobs, but for really big ones you may want to consider hiring a professional, right, with a commer-cial-duty rig.

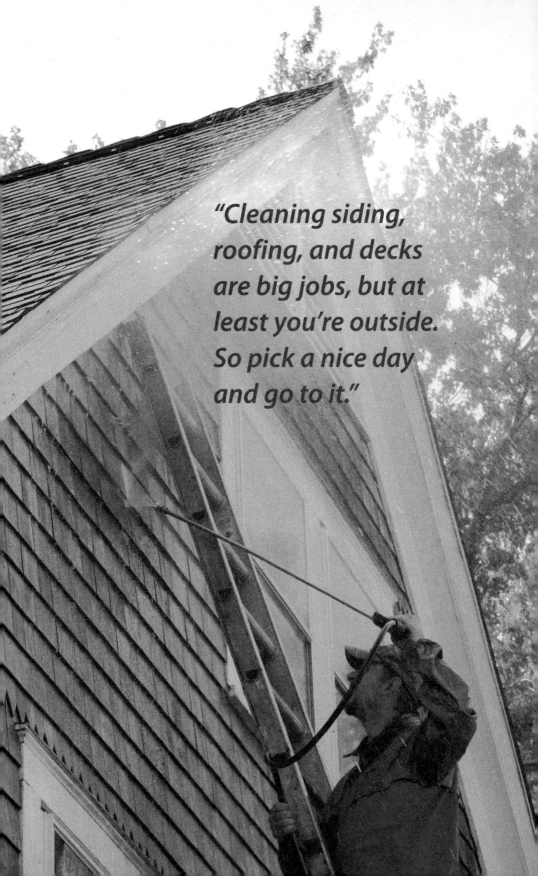

"Cleaning siding, roofing, and decks are big jobs, but at least you're outside. So pick a nice day and go to it."

It's no secret: the more frequently you clean siding, the easier it is to clean. But that doesn't mean you have to hose off the house every Saturday—most siding will look good if you clean it once a year. Choose a warm, sunny day so the moisture is less likely to seep into the structure.

Vinyl Siding

For routine cleaning, the **All-Purpose Liquid Cleaner on page 39** works well. Add a tablespoon of borax for mildew protection. Try the cleaning method described on the opposite page.

Trim shrubs so that they are at least 2 feet from the house. This will improve access and air circulation and reduce the chance of mold.

Aluminum Siding

Follow the directions for vinyl siding, above, but exercise greater care when scrubbing because scratches in aluminum siding will show the metal underneath the finish. Aluminum siding can benefit from a twice-yearly cleaning.

Wood Siding

A thorough washing can revitalize a wood-sided house. Follow the directions for vinyl siding, but remember to caulk and repair any holes or cracks before you begin. While you're at it, take note of where the paint is peeling and where wood is warped so you can do the appropriate fixes.

Cleaning Siding

What you'll need: pressure washer or garden hose with a nozzle attached, cleaner, and a soft brush

Work in small sections using a pressure washer or a garden hose with a nozzle attached. Wet the area where you'll be working. Always spray the siding from above, not below, because water directed from the ground up can seep underneath the boards and cause damage.

New attachments for pressure washers make scrubbing down siding easier for homeowners.

*Spray the siding with the **All-Purpose Liquid Cleaner on page 39**—the quickest way is to use a car-wash kit that comes with a soap-dispenser hose attachment. Another option would be to use a long-handled brush and apply soapy water from a bucket. (Pressure washers usually come with soap dispensers and may have brush attachments.)*

Rinse. Don't let the cleaning solution dry on the house. If you can't remove stubborn grime, gently scrub the siding with a soft brush, such as the kind used for cleaning cars. Then rinse again.

Dealing with Mildew

For houses with serious mildew, look for environmentally friendly products containing oxygen bleach. Adding borax to your cleaning solution can also help kill mildew and prevent it from coming back. Mildew tends to thrive in moist, shadowed areas, so be sure to look for the root causes of dampness, such as leaky shingles, gutters, or siding; excess interior moisture; or trees growing too close to the house. Mildew also needs organic matter such as pollen to grow, so keeping siding clean will help.

Brick and concrete walls should always be saturated thoroughly with water before cleaning—if not, the cleaner will soak into the wall and cause stains. Soaking the wall with water prevents it from absorbing the cleaning solution. After presoaking, wash the brick with a mild cleaner such as the **All-Purpose Liquid Cleaner on page 39**. Add a tea-spoon of borax to help eradicate mildew. Scrub any stains with a fiber brush. (Wire brushes can damage mortar and brick surfaces.) Then rinse with clean water.

If you're using a power washer, take care that the high pressure doesn't blow out mortar and strip the surface of sand-faced bricks.

POWER WASHER PROS AND CONS

There is an ongoing debate about the use of power washers (also referred to as pressure washers) as green cleaning tools. After all, most are driven by a noisy, polluting internal combustion engine, and they use a lot of water. Also, if they are not operated properly, they can damage siding, roofing, and even some masonry surfaces. Gouging and scarring from using a pressure setting that's too high is the common complaint.

Used properly, however, power washers are helpful cleaning tools. They get big jobs done quickly. Rent one annually and use it on siding, patios, decks, garage floors, driveways, and walkways. Heavy-duty machines are driven by 4- to 12-horsepower gasoline engines and can generate pressures well in excess of 3,000 pounds per square inch (psi) and water volumes over 4 gallons per minute (gpm). Electric units are also available but typically produce half the pressure and deliver far fewer gpm to the surface you're trying to clean. They are, of course, easier to use and produce less pollution on site. However, they are better suited to washing cars and trucks than cleaning the exterior of a house.

For many jobs, cleaning with just water is enough. When you do need a detergent, use one that's biodegradable, and then flush the surrounding area with plenty of clear water to disperse the detergent and prevent harm to shrubs and gardens. Never use bleach or a bleach-based product with a power washer. In addition to being harmful to you and your vegetation, it may damage the power washer's water pump.

Finally, never use more pressure than needed to get the job done. Test-clean a small, inconspicuous area before you begin to see if the pressure is too high. You'd be surprised. Sometimes hose pressure is sufficient to perform many cleaning tasks.

Muriatic, or hydrochloric, acid is frequently recommended for cleaning masonry and removing efflorescence. What isn't often mentioned is that muriatic acid is corrosive to human tissue, deadly to the environment, and officially regulated by the Environmental Protection Agency as a toxin.

Dealing with Stains

Unfortunately, oil and other stubborn stains are sometimes difficult to coax off of concrete or brick. First try a vinegar-water solution or a washing soda-water solution composed of equal parts of each. Apply it to the affected areas; scrub; let it sit for ten minutes; and then rinse it. Repeat several times.

There are also nontoxic commercial cleaning products available. Before using one, test it on a small, inconspicuous surface; bricks, in particular, can react unpredictably to different cleaning agents.

Presoak brick walls with water before cleaning.

Stucco

Patch any holes in the stucco before cleaning. Using a garden hose with a nozzle attached, wet the stucco from the bottom to the top. Presoaking the stucco prevents the dirty water from being absorbed. Start at the bottom and work up from there. After the stucco is presoaked, work top to bottom, spraying the surface with a mild soap-and-water solution such as the **All-Purpose Liquid Cleaner on page 39**. Add borax for mildew protection. Stubborn stains can be treated with oxygen bleach-based products. Rinse again until clean.

Water pressure alone is sufficient for many outdoor cleaning jobs, including wood and vinyl fences.

Efflorescence

Efflorescence is the name for those ugly white stains that occasionally appear on brick and concrete. They're caused by water and soluble salts that are trapped behind the wall and are trying to force their way to the surface. When they succeed, they show up as white crystalline residue. Efflorescence can be washed or scrubbed with a fiber brush, but it will reappear if its water source still exists. When the water dries, the efflorescence stops. If the white stains persist, the problem, and the solution, lie somewhere behind the wall, not on its face. To reduce the risk of efflorescence, don't wash brick or concrete surfaces in cool or damp weather. And avoid casually wetting brick or concrete—keep lawn sprinklers aimed in the other direction.

"A metal roof is on my wish list—it's low maintenance, long lasting, and recyclable."
—J.S.

ROOFING

A roof's material dictates everything else: how you clean it, how often you replace it, how much air conditioning you use—in short, how environmentally friendly it is. Here's an elementary eco-guide to roofing materials:

Asphalt: Waste is the key problem with asphalt roofing. Every time you re-roof, you're adding asphalt shingles to the landfill, and the most popular and affordable type lasts for only 15 years. If you buy asphalt shingles, choose a long-lasting brand. (Sometimes you can install shingles over old ones, but that's only delaying things.) They're also often treated with chemicals that release toxic VOCs into the atmosphere. Asphalt roofs require periodic cleaning—see "Shingles" on page 173—and individual shingles will occasionally crack or come loose. New shingles can be renailed or reattached with few problems by using roofing cement.

Wood: Wood shakes, which are frequently made from cedar, are usually cut from logs that are salvaged from logging operations. They're much more expensive than asphalt shingles, but with proper care they will last longer—as long as 50 years in ideal conditions. But proper care is critical. Wood shakes require far more maintenance than

[smart tip]

Replanting

If your roof and siding have chronic mold problems, consider relocating any shrubs and trees that are too close. Creating a clear space of a few of feet can substantially reduce the risk of mold and rot.

Prevention

The most low-maintenance way to keep a roof clean is to reduce what falls on it. Leaves, branches, and other detritus from surrounding trees are the source of many mildew and mold messes. If you have trees that hang over your roof, you may be able to trim them yourself or hire a professional service. Dried leaves can sometimes be controlled with a leaf blower. Avoid using a rake for removing leaves and branches because it can damage shingles. Special rakes are available for pulling snow off the roof.

asphalt shingles, and in moist and high-humidity climates they're susceptible to mildew and can rapidly decay. They need to be sealed for protection against mold and rot. For maintenance, see "Cleaning Shingles" on the opposite page. Broken or displaced wood shakes can be replaced and renailed.

Slate: Slate lasts for a long time—manufacturers like to say that it lasts as long as the structure. It can be bought used, but you should confirm that your contractor knows how to install salvaged slate. Slate is largely low maintenance, but have it inspected periodically to check for problems. Slate is tricky to repair and often suffers from faulty workmanship, so slate roofs should only be repaired by specialists.

Metal: Once only seen on industrial buildings, metal is now a widely available and increasingly popular alternative. Your house won't look like a warehouse: metal roofing can now mimic other materials such as slate or cedar. It's also an environmentally attractive option. Metal roofs will last at least 50 years—that's two to three times as long as an

SHINGLE RECYCLING

Our landfills are piled high with old asphalt shingles. According to the Environmental Protection Agency, roof installation is estimated to generate 7 to 10 million tons of asphalt-shingle waste annually. But there may be a market for old asphalt shingles on the horizon. A few companies are starting to recycle them into paving material. It's a potential win-win-win: roofers reduce their waste costs; pavement contractors reduce their material costs; and we reduce our landfill waste. If you're replacing an asphalt roof, see if a recycler in the area will take your old shingles. For more information, visit shinglerecycling.org.

asphalt roof. And metal roofs are frequently made out of recycled material and can be recycled again when they finally wear. Shiny metal is reflective, keeping house temperatures cool. Metal requires almost no maintenance beyond an occasional inspection.

Tile: An ancient roofing material, clay tiles have been used for thousands of years. Extremely durable and largely low maintenance, clay tiles can last for the life of a house, but

[smart **tip**]

Roof Safety

If your roof is low, preventative maintenance can be done from the ground. For higher roofs, exercise extreme caution. Ladders should extend one-fourth of their length from the wall and several rungs above the roofline. Needless to say, they should sit solidly on the ground. Avoid the upper rungs and keep your body within the sides of the ladder—don't reach. Climbing on roofs is extremely dangerous and should be done with a safety harness. In general, crawling around on roofs is best left to the professionals.

Cleaning Shingles

Power washers are often recommended for roof cleaning. However, if you have an asphalt-shingle roof, don't use one. (Power washing can be used successfully on wood shingles prior to resealing.) Unless used with care, they are likely to cause further damage. Few asphalt shingles are designed to stand up to strong water pressure. (If you do power wash, use the lowest setting and a nozzle that fans the water, ideally at 40 degrees.) A garden hose with a spray attachment is a smarter choice. As with siding, use the **All-Purpose Liquid Cleaner on page 39.** For advice on eliminating black algae stains, see the "Black Roofs" sidebar on page 174. If you are working on the roof, remember to spray water and apply cleaners from the top down. Aiming water up at the roof can tear off or damage shingles.

BLACK ROOFS

Look around at the roofs in your neighborhood and you'll likely see more than a few with black streaks across them. That isn't soot or dirt. It's actually an algae, *Gloeocapsa Magma*, that thrives on moisture and calcium carbonate, a component in many limestone-based asphalt shingles. *Gloeocapsa Magma* used to thrive in the humid South, but in the last few decades the algae has adapted and migrated across the United States, often appearing in the shaded sections of roofs. It's a seriously persistent stain and it can erode the surface of shingles and drastically shorten their life span. (The black surface also absorbs more heat during summer and raises temperatures.)

Instead of attacking the algae with chlorine bleach, which can damage shingles and corrode flashings and gutters, use oxygen bleach, the active ingredient in many environmentally friendly products. To prevent the algae from returning, install a strip of zinc or copper on your ridgeline. When it rains, the strip will leach minute quantities of the metal, which will coat the shingles and inoculate the roof against further growth.

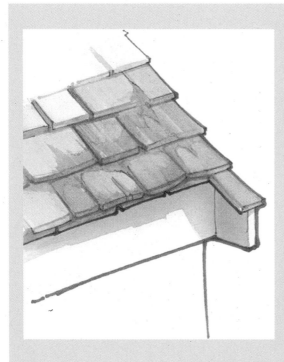

Moss

The oxygen-bleach method discussed in the "Black Roofs" sidebar above will also remove most moss. For any remaining moss, scrub the shingles in a downward direction. Moss has shallow roots and should fall off easily. To prevent moss from returning, use the zinc or copper strips described in the same sidebar.

when used in climates with extreme temperature swings, can deteriorate from freezing and then thawing. They should be inspected from the ground yearly. Any loose or missing tiles should be replaced. Concrete and plastic clay-tile look-a-likes are available, too, and are cheaper than clay. A few manufacturers now make plastic tiles entirely out of recycled materials.

Gutters

Cleaning gutters is unappetizing work, but there are few tasks that make a bigger difference to the condition of your home. Clogged or malfunctioning gutters can cause water stains, wet basements, and foundation damage. Try to clean gutters twice a year, and don't do it immediately after a rain—it'll be easier when the leaves are dry.

From the highest point on the gutters—see the "Roof Safety" Smart Tip on page 173—use rubber gloves to scoop out the accumulated gunk. When the gutter is unobstructed, flush it with water from a garden hose. Check that the downspouts are securely attached and that the water is directed away from the foundation.

For cleaning the outside of discolored metal gutters, use a biodegradable detergent and a coarse scrubbing pad on stubborn stains. Otherwise, an occasional blast from the hose or from a power washer should do the trick.

EXTERIOR METALWORK

Metalwork on railings, gates, and other structures can corrode quite quickly. Although toxic agents are frequently recommended for cleaning metals, there's no reason to resort to them. Stick with the wide array of tried-and-true, nontoxic household metal cleaners described on page 120. Consider allowing copper and bronze to keep their natural (and attractive) patina. For rusted metals, nontoxic rust removers are now available. If you have painted-metal items that need to be stripped, look into nontoxic vegetable-oil-based paint strippers. (For more information, see Resources.) Use jojoba or castor oil to lubricate squeaky hinges, sticky latches, and so forth.

7 Exterior Improvements to Reduce Interior Mold

2. Regularly inspect roof flashing at valleys, chimneys, and vent stacks.

1. Install attic vents at ridges and soffits, or in gables.

3. Clean gutters regularly, and keep downspouts clear.

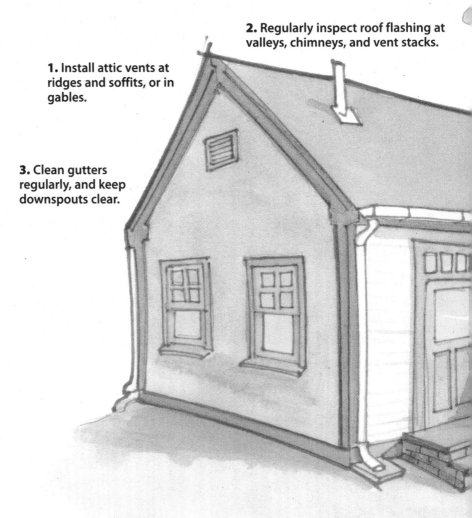

4. Slope grade away from the house.

5. Install a chimney cap to reduce rainwater infiltration.

6. Keep shrubs at least 2 feet from siding, and don't plant trees near sewer lines.

7. Use splash blocks to divert rainwater from the foundation.

Decks are exposed to the elements and to lots of foot traffic, so they get dirty—which means they require cleaning. Your cleaning duties will depend on the type of decking material—wood, synthetic, or aluminum.

Wood Decks

For many years, the heartwood from redwood or cedar was the standard choice for decks. Prized for its beauty and natural ability to resist rot, it has become increasingly rare, expensive,

DECKS VERSUS PATIOS

Wood Decks

- Higher maintenance
- Need to be thoroughly cleaned each year
- Should be resealed annually for protection
- Can rot or splinter
- Support fungal growth
- Usually made from a renewable resource

Synthetic and Aluminum Decks

- Less maintenance than wood decks
- Require no sealing
- Can be easily and effectively hosed
- Can use recycled materials
- Can be recycled

Masonry Patios

- Low maintenance
- Easy to clean
- May require replacement of stones or bricks
- If set in sand or grass, may shift and become uneven
- Last a lifetime

Decks are typically higher in maintenance but more versatile in design than patios.

Aside from weeds that sometimes grow in joints, masonry patios are nearly maintenance free.

and endangered. Today's redwood and cedar is often "new" growth and not from old forests. Both are suitable for deck building, but they will require more maintenance than your grand-dad's picnic table from the 1950s. To be sure that you're buying from an environ-mentally responsible lumber supplier, look for the seal of the Forest Stewardship Council (FSC).

Another popular decking material is pressure-treated wood. Pressure treating is now done with copper compounds, not arsenic. The treatment is highly effective, but you'll have to use a good water-resistant sealer to prevent the chemicals from leaching. (Note: this is especially impor-tant if you have an old pressure-treated deck preserved with compounds that include arsenic.)

[smart tip]

Brighter Deck Cleaning

In recent years, a shelf's worth of new products for deck cleaning and protection have appeared— especially for eliminating stub-born stains or brightening the wood's appearance. With so many environmentally friendly alternatives, toxic oxalic acid, the traditional solution for these problems, can easily be avoided. Look for products with either citric acid or oxygen bleach and follow label directions. (See Resources.)

Maintaining Wood Decks

Inarguably, the best way to keep a wood deck clean is to eliminate debris. Regular sweeping will save you time, add to the deck's life span, and mitigate any stains or mildew. If your deck boards have spaces between them, use a putty knife to scrape or push out any dirt, and then vacuum the deck with a shop vac to lift debris out of the cracks. (Choose a day when it's been dry for a while so the debris isn't wet.) The lessons of roof maintenance apply to decks, too: the fewer leaves and branches overhead, the less potential for decay. And when it snows, don't forget to sweep or shovel the deck. Moisture is a deck's enemy, and snow can damage untreated wood.

Redwood decks are beautiful and long lasting, but they require annual cleaning and sealing to maintain their appeal.

Plywood decks offer an interesting alternative to lumber decks. They can be coated with an acrylic polymer for a long-lasting, low-maintenance finish. In addition, plywood is a more efficient use of wood resources and is easier to install and maintain.

When your wood deck requires more than a routine cleaning (see below), the standard advice is to power wash it at high pressure and apply oxalic acid, which cleans and brightens the it. In most cases you can skip the acid. Use a biodegradable detergent instead. Pressure washing, even without the cleaner, works well on decks if done with care. Exercise caution, however, when selecting the pressure level. Too

Plywood decks can be coated with an easy-to-maintain acrylic polymer. Sand is added to the coating for traction.

high and it's easy to strip wood of its natural layer of protection, hastening its deterioration. The force of a power washing can even cause splintering. Also, do not use a pressure washer to strip paint from a deck because it can damage the wood.

Cleaning Wood Decks

For routine cleaning, rinse the deck with a hose, concentrating on the cracks between the boards where mildew and rot often begin. Then treat the deck with a mild cleaner such as the **All-Purpose Liquid Cleaner on page 39** and scrub the surface with a long-handled brush, working parallel to the wood's grain. Add a tablespoon of borax for any mildew. Grease stains can be treated by adding washing soda. Wait a few minutes, and then rinse the deck. Work in small sections.

Protecting Wood Decks

Before sealing, decks should be treated with the citric acid or oxygen-bleach products described in the "Brighter Deck Cleaning" Smart Tip on page 179. But what to use for sealing? Longtime oil-based sealers often contain VOCs, which can be toxic to you and the environment. But without a proper sealant, decks will deteriorate from water and sun damage. Luckily, there's a less-toxic solution: plant-oil-based sealers. If you use a synthetic sealant, study the label. Stay away from ethylene glycol and choose propylene glycol, which has far fewer VOCs. Redwood and cedar decks are sometimes left to fade naturally; both woods will weather elegantly.

Synthetic Decks

Synthetic decking is made with various types of virgin or recycled plastics, including high- and low-density polyethylene and vinyl. These plastics are often combined with other materials,

When using a pressure washer on any surface, exercise caution to avoid gouging and splintering.

Aluminum decking is easy to clean and can be recycled, should the need ever arise.

products, while similar in performance, are more environmentally damaging in their initial manufacture. Although synthetic decks are not made from renewable resources, there's no doubt that they will be easier to clean in a green, responsible manner. Think of the gallons of sealers, stains, and cleaners you'll save! In addition, lumber made only from plastic will be much easier to recycle in the future.

such as glass or wood fibers, to become what's called composite decking.

Polyethylene plastics, often recycled from products such as milk containers, make the most environmentally sound decking products. Vinyl-based lumber

Aluminum Decks

Aluminum makes an excellent, surprisingly strong—it rarely dents—material for decks. It's extremely low maintenance—a yearly rubdown with water and liquid soap should be adequate.

Cleaning Synthetic Decks

Composite decks have numerous attractive features. They won't rot or splinter, and they're largely maintenance free. They can be cleaned with a mild soap and water, and there's no need for sealing. But composite decks will fade over time, dulling their finish. Because their composition is partially wood, they are not impervious to mildew or mold, although they are far less sensitive than wood decks. When washing, spray through any cracks to remove any lingering organic material. A brisk scrubbing with a fiber brush should restore their shine. For grease stains, scrub the spots with a paste of washing soda and water, and then rinse clean.

Solid-plastic decks can be cleaned in the same manner as composites. They're equally easy to maintain—or even easier. Plastic decking should never mildew, for example.

Synthetic decks and railings wash clean with a light brushing and rinse. No sealers are required.

Maintenance of the hard surfaces outside your home varies depending on the material. As always, the best advice is to keep the surfaces free of debris and standing water.

Driveways and walkways made of concrete can be cleaned with the same methods used for brick and concrete walls. (See page 168.) A mild solution such as the **All-Purpose Liquid Cleaner on page 39** is best for basic cleaning. For oil or other stains, soak the area with equal parts vinegar and water or washing soda and water, and then scrub with a nylon or fiber brush. If the oil loosens, soak it up with a cloth and dispose of it; don't let it trickle down into the groundwater. If the stain persists, try an oxygen bleach-based product. Power washing works great on concrete because it's difficult to damage—although extremely high-pressure streams can scar it—and power washers can be effective on otherwise tough stains. For fixing cracks, use a nontoxic, zero-VOC filler. Several brands are available in home centers.

Tile and brick patios as well as stone and asphalt pavers can be cleaned and spot treated in the same manner as driveways. The reaction of each type to different cleaners varies, however, so test any product in an inconspicuous area. Avoid using an acidic cleaner on stone patios, and be careful about what you put on tiles—strong cleaners can

Brick is another low-maintenance patio material that is relatively easy to clean and maintain.

strip off a sealant. Avoid power washing, too, because any strong, direct stream of water can dislodge bricks or stones set in sand. Patios that are loosely fixed—set in sand or grass instead of mortar—should be occasionally weeded. No chemical cleaning treatments are necessary.

[smart **tip**]

Get Permeable

If your driveway needs replacing, consider switching to a permeable pavement. Conventional driveways catch water and funnel it into already overworked sewers. In a storm, less water runoff from driveways can prevent a sewage system from overflowing and polluting the environment. Permeable pavements can be made of asphalt, concrete, gravel, cement pavers, and grass.

Natural flagstone is as close as it comes to zero maintenance.

There's no reason to use toxins for cleaning patio and outdoor furniture. A little attention—there's no need to be fanatical—and mild soap and washing soda will do the job.

Placement and Storage

The best way to keep your outdoor furniture clean is to prevent it from getting dirty in the first place. When arranging your furniture, take note of environmental conditions that can cause dirt and deterioration, including:

• Overhead trees (drop pollen, insect honeydew, leaves, and bird droppings)

• Too much direct sun (dries wood and fades colors)

• Too much shade (encourages mildew growth)

• Rain (wears away any protective coatings)

Provide furniture protection from the elements whenever possible. Periodically rotate furniture from protected to unprotected areas.

And don't avoid the mundane tasks of covering and storing your furniture. Once the autumn weather becomes inclement and leaves begin falling, move furniture into a garage, basement,

Outdoor Furniture

Plastic furniture: Wipe down with the **All-Purpose Liquid Cleaner on page 39.** For tough stains, add a tablespoon of washing soda. Let it set for 10 minutes. Scrub with a soft brush, and then rinse.

Wicker furniture: Wipe down with warm water and a mild liquid soap. Rinse. Wash wicker furniture on a warm day so it dries quickly. Wet wicker will degrade faster.

Wooden furniture: Lightly wipe (don't soak) with warm water and an all-purpose liquid cleaner. For

mildew, add borax. Rinse.

To protect the wood, use a non-toxic wood sealer or wax. (See Resources.)

Aluminum and wrought-iron furniture: Wipe down with warm water and a liquid soap. (Do not use baking soda or washing soda because they can potentially discolor aluminum.) Rinse. Be careful with brushes, which may scratch the surface. Wiping with a solution of one part vinegar to one part water will help restore aluminum's shine. Carefully sand off any rust stains.

Today's outdoor furniture can stay out in rainy weather and dry quickly. Clean it with a soft brush.

or shed. Clean and dry items thoroughly first. Follow the same procedure for umbrellas and awnings. If you're short on space, buy breathable outdoor covers, which protect furniture far better than makeshift tarps. They'll fit snugly and keep moisture out, which prevents mold from forming.

Outdoor Fabric

Brush off umbrellas, awnings, and furniture cushions frequently to prevent dirt and grime from collecting. Regular washing removes the dirt and oil that encourages mold and discoloration. For spring and fall cleaning, rinse; dowse with water and a mild liquid soap; and then rinse again. Any outdoor furniture that's covered with fabric can receive the same treatment. Be sure to set the fabric out in the sun afterward so that it dries thoroughly.

Like outdoor furniture, grills will become unattractive and eventually unusable if they aren't protected from the elements.

Grill covers are the no-work solution. Many manufacturers provide a cover when you buy a grill. If your grill doesn't come with a cover, invest in a heavy-duty vinyl cover with a nylon lining. You don't want your cover getting blown off on a windy day, so get one with adjustable tabs, snap closures, zippers, or a drawstring to ensure a snug fit.

Grill Cleaning

To remove dirt and bird droppings from the surface, simply wash with the **All-Purpose Liquid Cleaner on page 39** and warm water.

Cleaning grill grates often involves nothing but heat and a grill brush. The heat of the grill does the work for you, incinerating a lot of what's left inside. After each use, when the coals have died down but the grill is still warm, scrub the grate with a stiff wire grill brush—the bits of food should flake off. Oil the grate lightly with olive oil. If the grill is dirty before you begin cooking, turn it on, close the lid, and wait 10 minutes. Then scrub the grate and wipe with olive oil.

GRILL CLEANING TIPS

1. Use a salted lemon to soften built-up grease from grates. The grill can be warm or cool.

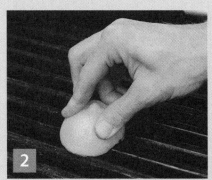

2. After rubbing the grate thoroughly with the salted lemon, wait several minutes before scrubbing.

A grill that's kept under cover will be much easier to clean—and will last longer, too.

3

For yearly cleaning, soak the grates in a tub of warm water and washing soda—overnight if necessary.

4

Scrub the grates with a mesh pad, and wash with liquid soap and water.

Garage, Workshop, and Basement

My home is definitely a work in progress. My husband and I have been renovating it for over 10 years. At first we were just aiming to make it more comfortable, but as time went on we started focusing on making it greener as well.

As a result of all our work, our garage and basement see a lot of use. We have construction materials, power tools, and supplies everywhere. We've moved away from using toxic chemicals, and we've made the time to take the old toxins to our hazardous-waste collection site. Don't delay in doing this. The faster they are out of your house, the less chance that they will poison your air—or your child or pet. Green up these areas today!

A clean garage floor, left, will help keep your house clean, too. Garage and workshop cleaning methods and products are another source of toxins. Even something as simple as how you clean your brushes, right, can make a difference.

"For many homes, the garage and basement are where toxins are making their last stand."

Most garage floors are concrete and just need occasional mopping to maintain them. Simply mop with the **All-Purpose Liquid Cleaner on page 39,** and then rinse the floor. (For more information, see "Driveways, Walkways, and Patios" on page 186.) Scrub any remaining dirt using a brush and a paste of baking soda and water. Ventilate the garage thoroughly after any washing— prompt drying will lower the risk of mildew. Remember to seal the garage floor to prevent water damage and cracking. Nontoxic, non-VOC sealers are available in either plant-based or polymer formulas.

Cleaning Oil Spots

Garage floors are frequently polka-dotted with oil stains—combating them can seem pointless. But there's a good reason to fight the good fight: if you don't, you'll never know whether a piece of equipment started dripping last week or last year. For light stains, soak the area with equal parts water and vinegar or water and washing soda, and scrub vigorously. Fresh oil stains can be treated with kitty litter, which is absorbent. Scatter the litter over the stain, and let it sit for a day. Sweep the area, and scrub using the vinegar or washing soda method described above. Then rinse. (Resist using sawdust, which can catch fire, in place of kitty litter.)

Of course, the easiest way to keep oil stains off the floor is to catch the oil before it hits the concrete. Position a paint pan filled with kitty litter or sand where oil stains tend to appear.

Pressure washing is the easy way to clean garage floors, assuming you have a floor drain.

When using newspaper to clean a windshield with vinegar, fold the paper into a pad for best results.

CARS

You'd never know it from the aisles of cleaning products in stores, but cars aren't particularly complicated to clean. If your car was just towed out of a swamp, you might have a problem. If not, car cleaning can rely almost exclusively on the ingredients and recipes introduced in Chapter 2.

Do-It-Yourself Washing

Avoid using commercial detergents. They're often too harsh for a car finish. Instead, use a half-cup liquid soap per

Bugs, Tar, and Tree Sap

Dead bugs aren't just unattractive. They're acidic, and that acid can eat away at a car's paint and coating. Remove bugs and all other types of goo from your car as soon as possible. Try scrubbing gently with the **Baking Soda Scrub on page 44.** If that doesn't work, try flax-seed oil, followed by careful scrubbing with a paste of baking soda and water.

THAT NEW-CAR SMELL

The smell of a new car is fresh and clean, right? In fact, recent studies have shown the exact opposite. That smell comes from VOCs found in plastics and used as fire retardants, and those chemicals have been linked to a wide range of illnesses. The first step when you buy a new car is to air it thoroughly. Heat will accelerate the off-gassing process, so park your car in the sun with all the windows closed and let it bake for the day; then open the windows and let the interior air thoroughly. Repeat for as many days in a row as needed until the strong smell dissipates. Always keep fresh air circulating in the car when you're driving. One way to avoid new-car off-gassing is to buy a used car with low mileage—off-gassing occurs mostly in the first six months.

Engines

The engine in any modern car is crowded with electrical components. Resist the temptation to rinse it—too many things can go haywire. A solution of washing soda and water can cut through the grease on many engines, but even if you use it carefully, it will likely wash oil into the sewers or groundwater. Professional garages can capture that oil and dispose of it properly. Trust them with it.

But you can selectively clean a dirty battery—the grime is draining some of the battery's power. Gently rub the battery's top and sides using a solution of baking soda and water. (For safety's sake, wear goggles when cleaning a battery. Sulfuric-acid explosions blind car owners every year.)

Once a battery has outlived its useful life, recycle it by bringing it to your service center or to a hazardous-waste collection site. Never toss an automotive battery into your household trash.

gallon of warm water and wash without a spray nozzle—the gentle sheets of water from a hose are more effective. Turn off the hose between rinses—as much as 150 gallons of water at a time are regularly wasted by people washing their cars—and move the car onto grass or gravel so the water is absorbed instead of running into the storm drains.

A simpler solution? Use a waterless car wash. These nontoxic formulas are simply wiped onto a car's exterior, where they absorb and dissolve dirt and grime. The best part is that wax is a part of the formula, so no separate waxing is necessary. Look for a product that is free of kerosene and silicone.

Air Filters

You may not know it, but driving with an old air filter is environmentally irresponsible. The gunk in any clogged air filter will cut down on gas mileage. Try to replace it every 15,000 miles.

Windshields and Windows

Windshields can be wiped off with a strong solution of vinegar and water (one part vinegar to two parts water). Use vinegar to clean the rest of your car windows as well, or use club soda instead—simply spray it on and wipe.

Green Fact

Tossing motor oil into the trash or pouring it down the sewer or on the ground is a crime. The oil in one car can contaminate a million gallons of water, according to the EPA. If you change your own oil, take the used oil to a collection center (often a gas station or auto-parts store).

Car Waxes

Recent regulations have lowered the amount of VOCs in car waxes. But these waxes still aren't like skin cream, and finding a nontoxic one isn't easy. Waxes made out of natural ingredients such as carnauba—a Brazilian palm tree—are still loaded with solvents. There are a few solvent-free commercial car waxes now available. (See Resources on page 218.) A waterless car-wash spray is another option. (See "Do-It-Yourself Washing" on page 195.)

Chrome sparkles after a simple polish with a rag and white vinegar. Lightly spray the surface with white vinegar, and then polish gently. Try rubbing rust spots with aluminum foil.

Undersides

Road salt and grime will eat away at a car's belly. The best prevention is to periodically spray underneath and wash the gunk out of wheel wells. This is best done at a car wash, where the runoff water will be caught and treated. Ask to make sure that your car wash does, in fact, spray the car's underside.

CAR WASH OR NOT?

There's a strong argument to be made that going to a car wash is more environmentally responsible than doing it yourself. Many car washes are legally bound to treat and reuse their wastewater, for example. (Regulations vary by state.) This way, they use less water because they're spraying it at a higher pressure. Studies have shown that businesses use from one-fourth to one-half less water than people do at home. And there are now eco-friendly car washes that use green cleaners, too.

Interiors

Dashboards: Whenever needed, dust dashboards using a microfiber cloth. To remove grime, all plastic surfaces can be wiped off with the **All-Purpose Liquid Cleaner on page 39.** If you're stuck without any, don't worry. A gentle rubbing with warm water and a rag should remove most dirt.

Floors: Use car mats. They can be clumsy and awkward, but cleaning rubber is far easier than cleaning carpet. Just take the mats out and vacuum them. If necessary, scrub with the **All-Purpose Liquid Cleaner on page 39** and rinse. For removing carpet stains that do occur, see page 145.

Seats and more: Fabric—including the fabric on the floor and the ceiling—can almost always be treated with a mild liquid soap and water. Simply wipe off the seats and let them dry. For stains, see the fabric-stain removal tips on page 142 and page 158. Cleaning vinyl seats is as easy as rubbing them with a wet rag. Buff leather with a liquid saddle soap, which will clean and condition at the same time.

If spills begin to smell—think spilled milk—a piece of white bread in a bowl covered with vinegar and left overnight should deodorize the car. (But don't forget to take them out before driving the next day!) Baking soda sprinkled on the odor's source should absorb it. Sweep or vacuum the baking soda later.

It's safe to bet that there is rust and grease on tools in almost every workshop—even though eliminating it isn't really difficult. Here are a few pointers.

Rust: Light rust will often fall off by rubbing with rough sandpaper or a stiff brush. For more stubborn rust, soak tools for a day in white vinegar. Then scrub using a wire brush, rinse, and wash with a mild soap and water. To prevent rust, keep tools clean and dry. Protect them from high humidity and moisture by storing them in a drawer with chalk or zeolite to absorb moisture. When appropriate, coat them with a nontoxic wax or paint.

Grease: Wash with the **All-Purpose Liquid Cleaner on page 39** with borax. Nontoxic degreasers are also widely available. Look for citrus- or hydrogen peroxide-based products. Use degreasers sparingly, and keep them out of reach of children. While green degreasers are better than the alterna-

Brush sawdust from tools after each use to avoid bigger cleaning jobs later.

"Even nontoxic paints and sealers have biocides in them to prevent mold growth and extend shelf life. If you are chemically sensitive, look for low-biocide paint or make your own milk paint or whitewash." – J.S.

tives, they are still powerful, so follow the manufacturer's instructions carefully.

Dust

Dust is the bane of woodworkers everywhere. Even if you only periodically cut or sand wood, fine dust grains are still accumulating in the air—an invisible hazard to your health. Breathing wood dust can cause serious respiratory problems. It isn't just a little cough that will subside. Wood dust from treated wood or composite products such as plywood can also contain hazardous chemicals. Professional woodworkers take this seriously. They have whole-shop dust-collection systems that trap even the finest particles.

For amateurs, the first rule is simple: open the windows. Good ventilation improves air quality and prevents mildew and rot. Vacuum any visible sawdust using a handheld vacuum. But if you're cutting wood more than occasionally, consider investing in a portable dust-collection unit, which attaches to whatever tool you're using. Its hood will suck up any dust before it can settle. When buying tools, choose those with integral dust-collection systems. It's always wise to wear a dust mask or respirator when you're working.

[smart **tip**]

Line That Tray

When using latex paint, line a sturdy metal paint tray with a tray liner. That way, you can throw away the liner when you're done, rather than waste water cleaning the tray.

Paint never ends up entirely on the object you're painting. How you clean up those extra spots depends on what paint you're using and where it has splattered. Fresh latex paint can be scrubbed off hard surfaces using just water. Soak spots on fabric right away in cold water, and then launder as usual. Soak old latex spots on hard surfaces with vinegar until they are softened Then scrub gently. If that doesn't work, try rubbing the spots with alcohol, with

CLEANING BRUSHES

1 *Whether cleaning acrylic, oil, or alkyd paint from a brush, first wipe thoroughly using a rag.*

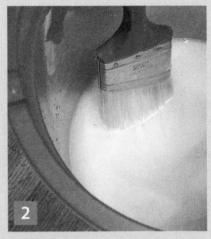

2 *Saturate bristles in water for an acrylic paint. Use a citrus-oil solvent for alkyd paints and oil paints.*

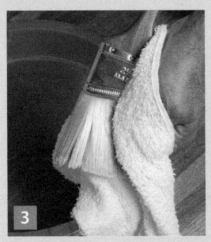

3 *Comb bristles and then wipe again using a clean rag.*

4 *If your paint session is interrupted, put the brush or roller in a plastic bag. It will keep for several days.*

vodka as the safest option. Be careful, though, alcohol can affect dyes.

Fresh alkyd-paint spills can be cleaned with citrus- or vegetable-based paint thinners now on the market. (See Resources on page 218 for more information.) Blot up as much as you can with a rag before going at it with thinner. Note that plant-based thinners are a less-toxic and environmentally sound option, but they should be used with caution. Use them in a well-ventilated area; dispose of them with other hazardous waste; and avoid skin contact.

Wrap Brushes for Breaks

If you're taking a break and are going to go back to painting within a couple of days, you don't need to clean your paintbrush or roller at all—you just need to prevent it from drying. Wrap the brush or roller in plastic wrap or aluminum foil; then place it in a sealed plastic bag. Place it away from any light source. When you're ready to paint, unwrap it. Store your brush in the freezer if you're breaking for longer than a day.

Cleaning Paintbrushes

Latex paints are water-based and are the best choice both from a health standpoint and ease of cleanup. Just a little liquid soap and water is all that is needed to remove old paint.

If you have a special situation that requires alkyd paint, you'll need to use a paint thinner. Traditional paint thinner is a noxious substance. In order to avoid it, some people recommend discarding brushes entirely. Tossing them, they say, is more environmentally sound than cleaning them. But as I mentioned above, there are new citrus-oil-based solvents that are much less toxic than

traditional ones. However, still use these products carefully.

First, wipe the wet brushes on a rag for several minutes. That will remove a surprising amount of the paint. Then put the paintbrush in a glass jar with a citrus-oil-based solvent and saturate the bristles. You may use a brush comb to help remove stubborn particles. Then wipe off as much solvent and paint residue as possible, using a rag before rinsing with water. Save the solvent that has been contaminated with the oil paint for reuse later. (See "Reusing Paint Thinner" on the next page.)

[smart tip]

Eco-Friendly Paint

Shy away from alkyd paints, and only buy latex paints that are labeled low- or no-VOC. Many major paint brands now have a low-VOC line. Also explore alternative paints and plasters made of natural ingredients, such as milk, clay, or vegetable or fruit oils.

Paint Disposal

No one ever buys exactly the right amount of paint. According to the EPA, as many as 69 million gallons of paint are left over annually. It's likely that your basement or garage is harboring a tiny fraction of that. Any amount of paint that's disposed of improperly—putting it in the trash, for example—can potentially contaminate soil and waterways.

The most eco-friendly option is to give away the paint. Check if any local organizations, such as the high school drama club or the local Habitat for Humanity chapter, might need extra paint. Or find an organization that blends it into new paint or recycles it into other products. (See Resources on page 218 for more information.) If that isn't available in your area, alkyd paint can almost always be disposed of on a hazardous-waste collection day or at a designated site. Regulations vary, so confirm with local officials. Allow leftover acrylic paint to solidify prior to disposal.

Both plant-based and petroleum-based paint thinners should also be disposed of with caution. Take them to a hazardous-waste collection site, too.

Before buying paint, use the manufacturer's guidelines to calculate how much you will need. This will minimize the possibility of extra paint you'll have to discard.

Reusing Paint Thinner

Reduce the quantity of used paint thinner you must discard by transferring it into a sealed container. (Glass or metal cans are fine, but make sure the cover has a tight seal.) Let it sit for a few days. The paint chips and other impurities will sink to the bottom. Later, pour the clear thinner on top into a separate container, and reuse. Discard the sediment as you would any hazardous waste.

Avoid spills when changing motor oil. Commercially available oil-collection containers help to conserve every drop and make recycling easier.

LAWN MOWERS

The lawn—and the mower that cuts it—are important status symbols in the average suburban community. Resist the urge to upgrade your lawn mower as often as you upgrade your computer. With good maintenance, a mower should last at least 7 years. Electric mowers, including battery-powered units, are greener and last longer. Regardless of your mower's condition, there's probably someone who can use it for parts when you're done, so be sure to give it away.

Maintenance

Most lawn-mower care is fairly easy and environmentally friendly. Use the tips below to make your lawn mowing more green and less stressful.

• **Sharpen blades yearly.** Dull blades damage grass and make your mower less efficient, which causes you to waste more time and gas on mowing.

• **Drain and replace oil yearly.** Do not throw or wash away old oil. Save it for hazardous-waste collection day or take it to a designated site.

Clippings

When you mow your lawn, leave your clippings where they fall—yard waste is estimated to take up between 10 and 20 percent of all landfill space. Most clippings are biodegradable and will enrich your grass. Grass clippings that are too long to decompose easily can be spread as mulch on your garden or composted. Leaves can also be used as mulch or compost. Your local municipal recycling facility may also take yard waste.

• **Gently wash a foam air filter,** if you have one, in a bucket with water and a small amount of nontoxic laundry detergent. Save the water—it'll be polluted with the oil—and dispose of it along with your used lawn mower oil.

• **Rinse the underside of the mower and wipe off wet grass clippings** or they'll stick. If clippings become caked on the mower, chip them off using a paint scraper or brush. Wash the underside occasionally with the **All-Purpose Liquid Cleaner on page 39.**

• **Scrub metal that's corroding** with baking soda and water or white vinegar and water. When the mower's retired for the season, be sure to wash and dry it thoroughly. Don't leave any residue or moisture that can turn into rust over the winter. Car wax can also be used on mowers to prevent rust. (Wax can be slippery, so avoid waxing the steps on riding mowers.)

Green Fact

According to the Environmental Protection Agency, more fuel is spilled each year filling up garden equipment than was lost in the entire Exxon Valdez oil spill in 1989. Add gas or oil to your mower on a flat, dry surface (a driveway or sidewalk, for example)—*not* when it's on the lawn.

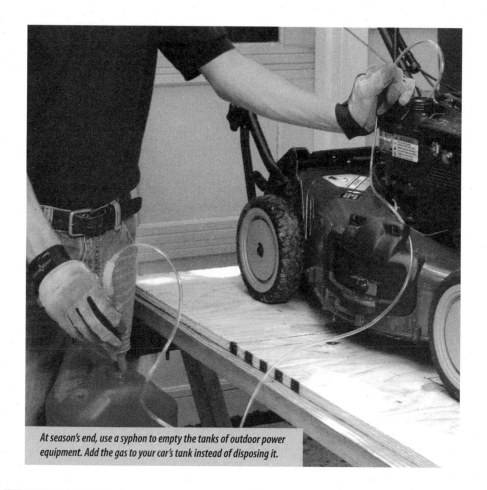

At season's end, use a syphon to empty the tanks of outdoor power equipment. Add the gas to your car's tank instead of disposing it.

PESTICIDES

In almost every garage, there are half-remembered, dust-covered bottles for waging war on lawn or garden pests. When you find them, remind yourself that throwing those bottles in the trash or emptying them down the drain is almost certainly environmentally irresponsible and possibly illegal. Like paints, these bottles should be treated as hazardous waste and disposed of at a hazardous-waste collection site.

Do yourself a favor and dispose of them sooner rather than later. The longer they sit in your garage, the greater chance they may get in the hands of small children. My family knows the dangers of pesticides firsthand: my grandmother's sister died at age 6 after eating an apple that had just been sprayed with pesticides.

It shouldn't be a surprise that basements are usually dank and moldy. After all, they're underground. But there are ways to determine what might be causing dampness, and you may be able to take steps to make things a lot more comfortable.

[smart tip]

Watch That Tank

If you use heating oil, note the age of your tank. (Most indoor tanks last about 30 years; most outdoor tanks last about 15.) Replacing an old tank before it leaks will save you one of the biggest and most-expensive cleaning headaches a homeowner can experience.

Diagnosing Basement Leaks

Moisture in a basement comes either from water that's formed inside (condensation) or water that sneaks in from outside (seepage). The sources of condensation and seepage aren't always easy to trace: air hitting cold windows, pipes dripping, or a shower or washing machine forming puddles. Seepage often stems from improper drainage outdoors—leaks during a rainstorm are a tell-tale sign.

To check if excess moisture is from condensation or seepage, tape a sheet of aluminum foil to an outside wall, being sure to seal all the edges completely. A day later, remove the foil. Water appearing on the outside of the foil is from condensation; water on the wall side is seepage.

Minor seepage can be treated with masonry sealer, for which there are now nontoxic options, including vegetable-oil-based sealants. Make sure that water is draining away from the house.

For condensation, consider insulating basement walls to

Mold

Mold can easily form from excess condensation. For cleaning it, use the **All-Purpose Liquid Cleaner on page 39** mixed with borax. (See "Mold and Mildew" in Chapter 3 for tips on preventing mold.) Anyone sensitive to mold should wear a mask when cleaning. Mold spores can be dangerous if they make the leap to heating and cooling ducts—from there, they can spread throughout a home. For serious mold remediation, contact a professional.

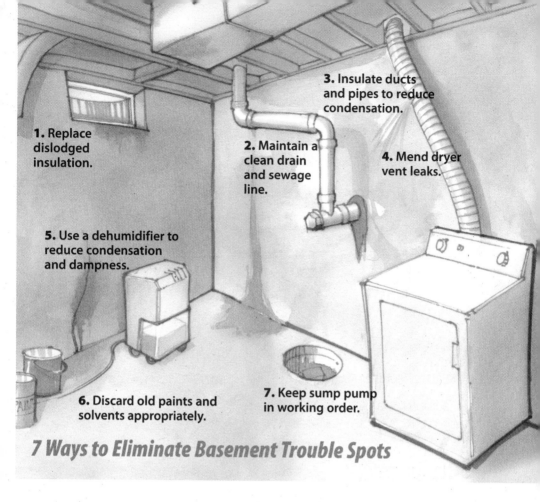

1. Replace dislodged insulation.

2. Maintain a clean drain and sewage line.

3. Insulate ducts and pipes to reduce condensation.

4. Mend dryer vent leaks.

5. Use a dehumidifier to reduce condensation and dampness.

6. Discard old paints and solvents appropriately.

7. Keep sump pump in working order.

7 Ways to Eliminate Basement Trouble Spots

prevent warm indoor air from touching the cold walls. Insulate all water-supply pipes, and be sure to track down and fix any leaks from pipes or appliances. Running a dehumidifier can also help control moisture. It will use energy, but it may be worth the cost if mold is causing health problems in your home.

Basement Floors

For tips on cleaning cement floors see "Driveways, Walkways, and Patios" on page 186. Consider sealing your basement floor to make it easier to clean—look for the nontoxic or vegetable-oil sealers mentioned earlier. Concrete finishes—which have traditionally relied on zinc, a heavy metal—are also available in nontoxic form. Look for Green Seal certification.

Cleaning After Flooding

The first lesson of flood maintenance is simple: get everything dry as fast as possible. Damp surfaces are a breeding ground for microorganisms, and high humidity increases the incidence of dust mites and mold, which can

[smart **tip**]

Drainage Check

Basement floors frequently suffer from poor drainage beginning at the roofline. It can never hurt to confirm that gutters are clean, downspouts are attached, and any water falling on the house is funneled away from the foundation. If necessary, strategically install a splash block to direct water away.

Then install dehumidifiers and air purifiers to reduce the risk of mold, mildew, and any long-term health problems.

When removing stains from carpets, avoid soaking spots. Treat topically with baking soda and water. Otherwise, look for hydrogen peroxide-based carpet cleaners. Items should dry quickly—ideally

provoke allergies.

After mopping any standing water, set up high-powered fans and open any windows to maximize ventilation.

after a day. If anything's still damp 48 hours later, toss it. Keep in mind that flood waters are potentially polluted, so limit your contact.

Efflorescence

Efflorescence is white residue that appears when trapped water forces its way through masonry. (For more information, see page 170.) Excessive efflorescence, especially on walls, is often an indication of a chronic moisture problem. Make sure that outdoor drainage is adequate and that the basement is properly ventilated. Superficially, efflorescence can be cleaned by scrubbing it with a mixture of white vinegar and water.

Efflorescence

Sewage Spills

Finally, there's the dreaded sewage backup. This usually occurs because of a blockage in the main sewer line to the street or septic tank, often due to a mass of fine tree roots. It can also be due to a blockage of a drain line in the house, often due to grease buildup, causing spillage through openings such as washing machine drainpipes and cleanout plugs. In both cases, you will probably need a plumber to clear the obstructions.

Dealing with the aftermath requires a perspective shift. You have to think about the damage you can't see. Sewage is a Trojan horse for disease, so wear water-resistant clothing, and take precautions. Relatively small overflows can be removed with a shop vac. That method will be too exhausting for larger spills, so call a professional, who will pump it out.

Disinfecting is absolutely necessary, but many commercial disinfectants have extremely toxic active ingredients. A vapor steam machine is a remarkable new alternative that disrupts the cells of microorganisms—even hospitals are now using these machines for disinfecting. (For more information, see page 49.) Discard anything that can't be thoroughly cleaned and disinfected.

Harmful Chemicals Found in Cleaning Products

This appendix is intended to provide more information on the specific chemicals found in cleaning products and the health problems they can cause. The sad fact of the matter is this is just the tip of the iceberg—there are so many chemicals in use now that it is virtually impossible to evaluate the risks of all the possible combinations. More than 85,000 chemicals are registered for use in the United States, and roughly 2,000 more are added each year. Those chemicals are used in more than 500,000 different products.

The following are the major health problems that have been linked to environmental toxins. As mentioned in Chapter 1, children are the most vulnerable to these toxins, and the effects of exposure are cumulative.

Cancer: The American Cancer Society expects rates of cancer to double by 2050. Perhaps exposure to chemicals does not account for all the increased cases, but most experts agree that environmental toxins do play a major role. The National Toxicology Program has identified 246 substances that are either "known carcinogens" or "reasonably anticipated to be a carcinogen"—and most of them are still legal and present in products we use everyday.

Asthma: Between 1980 and 1995, rates of childhood asthma doubled. Indoor air pollution, both at home and at school, has often been mentioned as a possible cause. The jump in the 1980s makes sense: after the energy crisis in the 1970s, new homes were built "tighter"—meaning they have less holes and cracks that leak air into and out of the house. This saves energy, but it means any chemical used in a building stays circulating in the air instead of getting flushed out by fresh air.

Immune and Reproductive Disorders: Hormone disrupters are chemicals that interfere with the body's hormonal or reproductive system. According to the United Nations, the effects of hormone disrupters may include ovarian, breast, testicular, and prostate cancers; reduced sperm counts in men; depressed immunity; a rise in early puberty; and impaired fetal development leading, possibly, to lower birth weight, reduced intelligence, hyperactivity, and violent behavior.

Learning and Behavioral Disorders:

A neurotoxin is any poisonous chemical that acts on the brain and nervous system. Neurotoxins can impair brain function and have been linked to decreased IQ and more learning disabilities, such as ADHD and autism.

List of Chemicals

When in doubt, avoid any ingredient ending in "-ene" or "-ol," or with "phenol," "chlor," or "glycol" in its name. And avoid products that say "Danger, Poison, Warning, Combustible, or Flammable."

Alkylphenol ethoxylate (APE): Synthetic surfactant is a hormone disrupter found in laundry detergents and all-purpose cleaners. It mimics estrogen and interferes with human reproduction and development.

Ammonia (ammonium hydroxide): A water solution of the gas, ammonia, it has an extremely sharp, irritating odor. Ammonia fumes are very irritating and corrosive to the eyes, nose, and airways. Fumes may cause a burning sensation, coughing, wheezing, shortness of breath, laryngitis, rhinitis, and watery eyes. Eye contact may cause severe eye burns, blindness,

cataracts, and glaucoma. Skin contact with low-ammonia concentrations may cause skin irritation; high concentrations will cause burns and open sores if not washed quickly. If swallowed in household cleaning products, it may cause burns in the mouth, throat, and stomach.

Benzene (benzol): Benzene is a known carcinogen and a volatile organic compound (VOC) used as a solvent in waxes, paints, and paint thinners. Exposure can lead to a decrease in red blood cells, and possibly cause anemia, bone-marrow damage, excessive bleeding, immune-system depression, and drying and scaling of skin. The effects of benzene on the central nervous system range from drowsiness, dizziness, and headaches to loss of consciousness.

Butyl cellosolve (ethylene glycol monobutyl ether): A neurotoxin and mutagen found in anti-freeze, all-purpose cleaners, window cleaners, spray cleaners, and scouring powders. Exposure can damage the liver, kidneys, and male reproductive glands, as well as cause harm to developing fetuses. An eye, nose, and throat irritant, it can cause headaches, dizziness, light-headedness, and confusion. It has been linked to learning disabilities among children.

Chlorine bleach (sodium hypochlorite): A severe irritant found in bleaches, scouring powders, toilet-bowl cleaners, dishwasher detergents, laundry detergents, and disinfectants. Household bleach is the most common cleaner accidentally swallowed by children. It is a development toxicant, meaning it can interfere with normal development of a fetus or child. It can cause severe skin and eye irritation or chemical burns to broken skin. Inhaled in high concentrations, it can cause respiratory problems including coughing, choking, chest pain, emphysema, and chronic and acute bronchitis. In laboratory animals, repeated inhalation of chlorine has damaged the liver, kidney, blood, heart, and immune and respiratory systems.

Dioxane (diethylene dioxide): A carcinogen and immunosuppressant used as a solvent in window cleaners, laundry liquids, and dish liquids. Exposure to high levels of dioxane can result in liver damage, kidney damage, and death. Eye and nose irritation was reported by people inhaling low levels of dioxane vapors for short periods. Studies in animals have shown that breathing, ingesting, or skin contact with dioxane can result in liver and kidney damage.

Formaldehyde: A known carcinogen found in air fresheners and disinfectants. It is a strong-smelling VOC and common indoor air pollutant. It can cause allergy-like reactions, such as watery eyes; burning sensations in the eyes, nose and throat; stuffy nose; and skin rashes. Allergic skin rashes and dermatitis may occur from skin contact with permanent-press clothing or other finishes that contain formaldehyde. It can also cause flu-like symptoms, such as headaches, nausea, and fatigue. Inhaling formaldehyde fumes can cause respiratory problems and asthmas-like symptoms.

Kerosene: A petroleum fuel oil found in furniture polishes and waxes that can damage the lungs and nervous system. Drinking small amounts of kerosene may cause vomiting, diarrhea, coughing, stomach swelling and cramps, drowsiness, restlessness, painful breathing, irritability, and unconsciousness. Drinking large amounts of kerosene may cause convulsions, coma, or death. Skin contact with kerosene for short periods may cause itchy, red, sore, or peeling skin.

Methylene chloride: A suspected carcinogen and neurotoxin found in air fresheners, degreasers, and paint strippers. Breathing in large amounts of methylene chloride can cause dizziness, nausea, and a tingling or numbness in fingers and toes. A person breathing smaller amounts of methylene chloride may become less attentive and less accurate in tasks requiring hand-eye coordination. Skin contact with methylene chloride causes burning and redness of the skin.

Napthalene: A carcinogen and neurotoxin found in toilet-bowl cleaners, carpet cleaners, deodorizers, and moth balls. Exposure to high concentrations of naphthalene can damage or destroy red blood cells, causing fatigue, lack of appetite, headaches, nausea, bloody or darkened urine, restlessness, a yellow or pale appearance, and in severe cases, kidney failure. Ingesting naphthalene mothballs can rapidly result in coma and death if not recognized and treated appropriately. Naphthalene fumes can irritate eyes, skin, and the respiratory tract. If inhaled, it can affect the central nervous system, causing headaches, confusion, nausea, fatigue, vomiting, sweating, and disorientation. Inhaling naphthalene fumes can cause brain damage in infants. Naphthalene has caused cancer in test animals inhaling it.

Perchloroethylene (perc): A carcinogenic and neurotoxic solvent widely used in dry cleaning. It can also be found in spot removers, rug and upholstery cleaners, water repellents, aerosols, adhesives, wood cleaners and polishes, and sealants. It easily evaporates, making it a common indoor air pollutant. Perc can irritate the eyes, skin, and respiratory tract and damage the liver and kidneys. Perc has caused cancer in animals. Results of animal studies suggest that perc can cross over the placenta to expose the fetus. If inhaled at high doses, it can affect the nervous system, causing intoxication, memory loss, confusion, dizziness, fatigue, drowsiness, headaches, nausea, weakness, and unconsciousness.

Phenol: A highly toxic poison found in furniture polishes and mold and mildew cleaners. Skin exposure to high amounts can produce burns, liver damage, dark urine, irregular heart beat, and even death. Ingestion of concentrated phenol can produce internal burns and death. Short-term exposure to phenol in the air can cause respiratory irritation, headaches, and burning eyes. In animals, exposure to high concentrations of phenol in the air for several weeks caused paralysis and severe injury to the heart, liver, kidneys, and lungs, and in some cases, death.

Sodium hydroxide (lye): A highly corrosive agent found in drain cleaners. It can cause severe burns upon contact. Inhalation of low levels of sodium hydroxide as dust, mist, or aerosol form may cause irritation of the nose, throat, and respiratory airways. Inhalation of higher levels can produce swelling or spasms of the upper airway leading to obstruction and loss of measurable pulse. Ingestion of solid or liquid sodium hydroxide can cause spontaneous vomiting, chest and abdominal pain, and difficulty swallowing. Corrosive injury to the mouth, throat, esophagus, and stomach is very rapid and may result in perforation, hemorrhage, and narrowing of the gastrointestinal tract. Skin contact with sodium hydroxide can cause severe burns with deep ulcerations. Contact with the eyes may produce pain and irritation, and in severe cases, clouding of the eyes and blindness. Death can result from shock, infection, lung damage, or loss of measurable pulse.

Stoddard solvent: A neurotoxin found in degreasers and spot removers. Exposure to Stoddard solvent in the air can affect the nervous system and cause dizziness, headaches, or a prolonged reaction time. It can also cause eye, skin, or throat irritation. Rats, cats, and dogs that breathed in large amounts of Stoddard solvent for several hours suffered seizures.

Synthetic dyes: Synthetic dyes are generally made from petroleum or coal tar (a carcinogen). Due to their manufacturing process, they may carry toxins, such as benzene, or heavy metals, such as mercury. They are often skin irritants and toxic to aquatic life. There are approximately 1,200 dyes used in household products.

Synthetic fragrances: Fragrances have long been recognized as skin allergens and irritants, and they are increasingly cited as a trigger in health conditions such as asthma, allergies, and migraines. In addition, some fragrance materials have been found to accumulate in the body and are present in breast milk. Other materials are suspected of being hormone disrupters. Fragrances are VOCs, which contribute to both indoor and outdoor air pollution. Synthetic musk compounds are persistent in the environment and contaminate waterways and aquatic life.

Toluene (methylbenzene): A neurotoxin and developmental toxin found in adhesives, paints, paint thinners, lacquers, stain removers, and dyes. It can cause eye, skin, and respiratory irritation. If inhaled, it may depress the central nervous system, causing lightheadedness, headaches, euphoria, confusion, dizziness, drowsiness, memory loss, and, at higher concentrations, unconsciousness or death. It may also cause kidney and liver damage. Permanent brain damage can result from prolonged exposure, impairing speech, vision, and hearing, and causing loss of muscle control, memory, and balance. Exposure to high levels of toluene during pregnancy can damage fetal development.

Triclosan: An antibacterial found in sponges, dish soap, hand soap, and numerous other household products. One study has shown that it reacts with chlorinated tap water to form chloroform—a known carcinogen. Another study has shown that under certain conditions it can mix with sunlight and form dioxin which is a carcinogen. Several studies have shown that Triclosan is no better than plain soap and water when it comes to killing germs.

Turpentine: A strong-smelling, flammable solvent made from the resin and oil of pine trees. It is a neurotoxin used as a paintbrush cleaner and paint thinner. Turpentine is also an ingredient in some varnishes, waxes, and polishes. Exposure to turpentine vapors can irritate the eyes, nose, throat, and respiratory tract and may cause headaches, coughing, nausea, dizziness, and other symptoms. If swallowed, turpentine can cause burning and pain in the mouth, throat, and abdomen; nausea, vomiting, diarrhea, confusion, and stupor. Repeated or long-term exposure may damage the kidneys, bladder, and central nervous system and cause skin allergy and eczema.

Sources
Agency for Toxic Substance and Disease Registry (www.atsdr.cdc.gov)
Healthy Child Healthy World
(www.healthychild.org/resources/chemical)

The following list of manufacturers and associations is meant to be a general guide to additional industry and product-related sources. It is not intended as a listing of products and manufacturers represented by the photographs in this book.

Aerus LLC

5420 LBJ Fwy., Ste. 800
Dallas, TX 75240
800-243-9078
www.aerusonline.com
Offers a range of products for a healthy home, including HEPA vacuum systems, air purifiers, and furnace filters.

AFM Safecoat

3251 Third Ave.
San Diego, CA 92103
619-239-0321
www.afmsafecoat.com
A leading innovator in low-toxicity paint and building products to preserve indoor air quality. Safecoat® Products include paints, grout sealers, and household cleaners.

AllergyBuyersClub.com

486 Totten Pond Rd.
Waltham, MA 02451
781-419-5500
www.allergybuyersclub.com
Specializes in allergy-relief products, including vacuum cleaners, air purifiers, dehumidifiers, steam cleaners, and bedding. The Web site includes a Learning Center with healthy-living information. Topics include Indoor air quality, molds, dust mites, and toxins.

American Association of Poison Control Centers

3201 New Mexico Ave., Ste. 330
Washington, DC 20016
202-362-7217
www.aapcc.org
A nationwide organization of poison centers and interested individuals that promotes the reduction of morbidity and mortality from poisoning through public and professional education and scientific research.

American Cancer Society

P.O. Box 22718
Oklahoma City, OK 73123
800-ACS-2345
www.cancer.org
A nationwide, community-based voluntary health organization committed to fighting cancer. The Web site includes information on cancer rates and the impact of environmental carcinogens.

Andersen Corporation

100 Fourth Ave. North
Bayport, MN 55003-1096
800-426-4261
www.andersenwindows.com
Offers a full line of energy-efficient patio doors and windows, as well as insect screens and door and window hardware. The company's products are Green Seal® certified.

Arm & Hammer

Church & Dwight Co., Inc.
P.O. Box 7468
Princeton, NJ 08543
800-524-1328
www.armhammer.com
www.thelaundrybasket.com
Makers of baking soda and washing soda. Their Web sites provides tips for using these products throughout your home.

Aubrey Organics

4419 North Manhattan Ave.
Tampa, FL 33614
800-282-7394

www.aubreyorganics.com
Known for their 100 percent natural hair-care, skin-care, and body-care products, they also make a nontoxic household cleanser and a liquid glass cleaner.

Benefect
c/o Sensible Life Products
7 Innovation Dr., Ste. 34
Flamborough, ON, Canada L9H 7H9
800-909-2813
www.benefect.com
Sensible Life Products manufactures Benefect® Disinfectant, the first EPA-registered botanical disinfectant. It's suitable for use around children, pets, and those that are sensitive to chemicals. The patented technology is proven to kill over 99.9 percent of bacteria. The company also has a multipurpose cleaner and cleaners for carpets and surfaces that have been damaged by fire and smoke.

BE SAFE (Center for Health, Environment and Justice)
P.O. Box 6806
Falls Church, VA 22040
518-732-4538
www.besafenet.com/pvc/safe.htm
The Center for Health, Environment and Justice's BE SAFE campaign is a nation-wide initiative to build support for the precautionary approach to prevent pollution and environmental destruction before it happens. BE SAFE coordinates the PVC Consumer Campaign, which educates consumers and companies about PVC. The Web site includes information about safe, cost-effective alternatives to PVC.

Best Paint Co. Inc.
1728 Fourth Ave. South
Seattle, WA 98134
206-783-9938

www.bestpaintco.com
Produces zero-VOC, biocide-free paints and sealers.

Better Basics
www.betterbasics.com
A source for homemade cleaning solutions and recipes.

Bi-O-Kleen
P.O. Box 820689
Vancouver, WA 98682
800-477-0188
www.biokleenhome.com
Manufacturers nontoxic household cleaners and laundry products from soy and citrus extracts. The company doesn't test its products on animals and considers the environment in all its operations. Products are made from renewable resources and sold in concentrated form to limit packaging.

BioShield
3215 Rufina St.
Santa Fe, NM 87507
800-621-2591
www.bioshieldpaint.com
Manufactures products derived from natural and easily renewable resources without harmful chemicals, toxins, and additives. The company's product line includes paints, wood stains, and household cleaners.

Blue Wonder Corporation
c/o CWR Enterprises
1010 East 55th Ave.
Vancouver, BC, Canada V5X 1N9
888-343-2583
www.bluewondercloth.com
Produces and markets a line of environmentally friendly microfiber cleaning products, including a mopping system and Classic and Deluxe cloths in various sizes.

Bona

2550 South Parker Rd., Ste. 600
Aurora, CO 80014
800-872-5515
www.bona.com
Produces and sells a total system for hardwood-floor finishing and care, including floor polish, mop oil, dry floor cleaner, waxing equipment, and other floor-care products. Bona innovations in dust containment and low-VOC water-borne finishes have reduced the health and environmental hazards of hardwood-floor finishing.

Bon Ami

510 Walnut St., Ste. 300
Kansas City, MO 64106-1209
816-842-1230
www.bonami.com
Bon Ami nontoxic cleansers are easy to find at the grocery store and contain no chlorine, no perfume, and no dye. Its polishing cleanser contains a mild detergent. Its "1886 Formula Cleaning Powder" is their original formula with no detergent.

Breezecatcher Clothes Dryers

5 Beverly Crescent
Beverly Court
Knocklyon
Dublin 16 Ireland
011-353-1-494-5630
www.breezecatcher.co.uk
Produces high-quality clotheslines, including a top-spinner rotary model.

Center for Children's Health and the Environment

Mount Sinai School of Medicine
Box 1043
One Gustave Levy Pl.
New York, NY 10029
212-241-7840
www.childenvironment.org
Academic research and policy center that examines the links between exposure to toxic pollutants and childhood illness. Its mission is to protect children against environmental health threats.

Citra-Solv, LLC

P.O. Box 2597
Danbury, CT 06813-2597
203-778-0881
www.citra-solv.com
Produces citrus-based cleaning products without harsh chemicals or damaging petroleum distillates, including all-purpose cleaner, dishwashing liquid, dishwashing powder, laundry detergent, glass cleaner, furniture polish, spot remover and castile soap.

Clotheslines Inc.

1605 East Main St.
Fredericksburg, TX 78624
830-997-6044
www.clotheslines.net
Manufactures easy-to-install, energy-saving clotheslines for the garage. No drilling or special tools required. The clothesline does not interfere with the operation of the garage door.

Coastal Scents

935 Third Ave. North
Naples, FL 34102
239-214-0181
www.coastalscents.com
An online source for citric acid, which is used in the Dishwasher Powder recipe on page 41.

ConcreteNetwork.com

31776 Yucaipa Blvd., Ste. 3
Yucaipa, CA 92399
866-380-7754
www.concretenetwork.com
Comprehensive online resource—for homeowners and contractors—that

includes information on caring for and repairing concrete floors.

Consumer Product Safety Commission

4330 East West Hwy.
Bethesda, MD 20814
800-638-2772
www.cpsc.gov
Organization charged with protecting the public from unreasonable risks of serious injury or death from more than 15,000 types of consumer products.

Country Rose Soap Co. Ltd.

15633 Buena Vista Ave.
White Rock, BC, Canada, V4B 1Z3
604-535-1622
www.countryrosesoap.com
Manufactures 100-percent olive oil castile soap.

Country Save

19704 60th Ave. NE
Arlington, WA 98223
360-435-9868
www.countrysave.com
A company—founded in 1977 by Elmer Pearson, the inventor of Elmer's Glue—that produces environmentally safe powdered laundry detergent, liquid laundry detergent, bleach, and all-purpose cleaner. It is also committed to utilizing the most environmentally responsible packaging available.

Daddy Van's Furniture Polish

P.O. Box 3425
Evergreen, CO 80437
303-679-0096
www.daddyvans.com
Produces all-natural, solvent-free furniture polish, which is available unscented or scented with essential oils, such as lavendar.

Debra's List

www.debraslist.com
A Web site with links to thousands of products that are safe for human health and the environment. Categories include indoor air, babies and kids, body care, cleaning, food, and pets.

The Dial Corporation

15501 North Dial Blvd.
Scottsdale, AZ 85260
480-754-3425
www.dialcorp.com
Manufactures 20 Mule Team® Borax, a multipurpose cleaner used extensively in this book.

Diaper Pin

www.diaperpin.com
An online resource for advice, information, and reviews on cloth diapers.

Don Aslett's Cleaning Center

P.O. Box 6135
Pocatello, ID 83205
800-451-2402
www.cleanreport.com
An online source for cleaning tools, including vacuums, microfiber dust mops, shower squeegees, rubber brooms, upholstery brushes, and microfiber cloths.

Dr. Bronner's Magic Soaps

P.O. Box 28
Escondido, CA 92033
877-786-3649
www.drbronner.com
Manufactures liquid and bar castile soaps that are made with organic oils and certified under the USDA's National Organic Program. The company encourages sustainable agriculture, farm worker health, and ecological processing methods. All its bottles are made from recycled plastic.

Earth 911

http://earth911.org
A Web-based environmental company that provides recycling resources for paint, carpeting, and more.

Earth Friendly Products
44 Green Bay Rd.
Winnetka, IL 60093
800-335-ECOS
www.ecos.com
A leader in the development and production of environmentally friendly cleaning supplies for household and commercial use. Its product line, which can be purchased online or from various national retailers, includes all-natural dishwashing liquid, laundry detergent, and pet-care products. Every Earth Friendly product is cruelty free and biodegradable.

Eco-Logics, Inc.
14876 Scotchtown Rd.
Montpelier, VA 23192
804-283-6269
www.green-kits.com
Manufactures earth-friendly cleaning kits and gift baskets. The green kits include nontoxic household products, environmentally friendly paper and household goods, and organic baby and personal care products. Nontoxic cleaning products include all-purpose surface cleaners, laundry soaps, and dishwasher cleaners.

Eco Safety Products
1522 East Victory St., Ste. 2
Phoenix, AZ 85040
877-366-7547
www.ecosafetyproducts.com
Wholesale distributor of green building products, including nontoxic paints, paint strippers, and sealers.

EcoSolve Americas Inc.
70 Tetherwood Blvd.
London, ON, Canada N5X 3W3
866-435-2511
www.ecosolveamericas.com
Offers water-based paint strippers, paint brush cleaners, and related finish-removal products.

Eco Touch
1500A Lafayette Rd.
PMB #424
Portsmouth, NH 03801
603-305-5747
www.ecotouch.net
Sells a line of waterless car-wash products that are nontoxic, biodegradable, and petrochemical-free. The company strives to conserve water, eliminate contaminated runoff, and save time when cleaning the car.

Ecover
2760 East Spring St., Ste. 220
Long Beach, CA 90806
800-449-4925
www.ecover.com
An international company that produces ecological cleaning products, including dishwashing liquid, dishwasher tablets, laundry powder, and floor soap. Products are available online and in Whole Foods, Wild Oats, and other natural food stores nationwide. Ecover has extended its environmental policy to all company departments, from production to marketing.

Energy Star
1200 Pennsylvania Ave. NW
Washington, DC 20460
888-782-7937
www.energystar.gov
A joint program of the Environmental Protection Agency and Department of Energy that offers energy-efficient solu-

tions. Appliances (such as dishwashers and washing machines) that have earned the Energy Star label use less energy, save money, and help protect the environment.

Environmental Health Perspectives
c/o Brogan & Partners
14600 Weston Pkwy.
Cary, NC 27513
919-653-2581
www.ehponline.org
A monthly journal of peer-reviewed research and news on the impact of the environment on human health. EHP is published by the National Institute of Environmental Health Sciences, and its content is free online. Print issues are available by paid subscription.

Environmental Protection Agency (EPA)
Ariel Rios Building
1200 Pennsylvania Ave. NW
Washington, DC 20460
202-272-0167
www.epa.gov
A federal agency established in 1970. Its mission is to protect human health and the environment. The EPA's Web site includes a wealth of information on environmental toxins, indoor air quality, and household hazardous waste.

Environmental Working Group
1436 U St. NW, Ste. 100
Washington, DC 20009
202-667-6982
www.ewg.org
A nonprofit organization with a mission to use the power of public information to protect public health and the environment. The EWG specializes in providing useful resources to consumers while simultaneously pushing for national policy change. An excellent resource for in-

depth information on environmental toxins in household and beauty products of all kinds.

Euronet USA
131 Sky View Circle
Spruce Pine, NC 28777
828-765-9863
www.euronetusa.com
Source for microfiber cloths and mops.

FilterQueen
Health-Mor
13325 Darice Pkwy., Unit A
Cleveland, OH 44149
800-344-1840
www.filterqueen.com
Manufactures and sells indoor air-quality systems, including air cleaners and surface cleaners. The products are used to remove both surface and airborne allergens, dirt, and dust from home interiors.

FindCO2.com
www.findco2.com
A state-by-state directory of dry cleaners that clean with liquid carbon dioxide.

Forbo Linoleum Inc.
Humboldt Industrial Park
P.O. Box 667
Hazelton, PA 18201
570-459-0771
www.forbolinoleumna.com
Manufactures linoleum products that are produced from renewable materials: linseed oil, rosins, wood flour, jute, and ecologically responsible pigments.

The Freecycle Network
P.O. Box 294
Tucson, AZ 85702
www.freecycle.org
A private, nonprofit organization with more than 4 million members worldwide who, in an effort to reduce waste, save

precious resources, and ease the burden on landfills, give away (and receive) old items such as vacuums and washing machines instead of discarding them.

GreenBoatStuff.com

1003 West 21st Ave.
Spokane, WA 99203
866-535-1610
www.greenboatstuff.com
A source for cellulose sponges, natural scrub brushes, and other green cleaning products. The company strives to offer only products that will biodegrade in a reasonable period of time.

GreenerChoices.org

www.greenerchoices.org
A Web-based initiative launched in 2005 by the publisher of *Consumer Reports* to inform, engage, and empower consumers about environmentally friendly products and practices. The site offers information on buying greener products that have minimal environmental impact and meet personal needs.

GreenEarth Cleaning

51 West 135th St.
Kansas City, MO 64145
877-926-0895
www.greenearthcleaning.com
A company that has patented an environmentally friendly process that uses liquid silicone for dry cleaning. The Web site allows you to search for GreenEarth® cleaners in your area.

The Green Guide

National Geographic
432 West 45th St.
New York, NY 10036
212-598-4910
www.thegreenguide.com
A bimonthly publication (online and in print) by National Geographic Society

that provides information on a variety of everyday health and environmental issues. Topics include earth-friendly products, green living, organic food, food-safe plastics, and more.

GreenHomeGuide

www.greenhomeguide.com
A community-based resource that provides tips, case studies, articles, and regional directories of products and services to assist people who want to green their homes.

Green Mountain Soapstone Corporation

680 East Hubbardton Rd.
Castleton, VT 05735
802-468-5636
www.greenmountainsoapstone.com
Offers precision-crafted soapstone sinks, countertops, wall and flooring tiles, shower basins, cabinet knobs, and masonry heaters.

GreenPeople

425 South Third Ave., Ste. 1
Highland Park, NJ 08904
732-514-1066
greenpeople.org
An online directory of eco-friendly products, services, organizations, and events. It includes a service that allows you to search for health-food stores by zip code.

Green Seal

1001 Connecticut Ave. NW, Ste. 827
Washington, DC 20036-5525
202-872-6400
www.greenseal.org
An independent nonprofit organization that promotes the manufacture, purchase, and use of environmentally responsible products and services. The Green Seal® identifies a product as environmentally preferable. A list of certified

products can be found on its Web site, including cleaners, floor-care products, and paints and coatings.

Grist
710 Second Ave., Ste. 860
Seattle, WA 98104
206-876-2020
www.grist.org
A nonprofit organization that offers online news and commentary about green issues and sustainable living. The "Ask Umbra" column offers green product information.

Howard Naturals
560 Linne Rd.
Paso Robles, CA 93446
800-266-9545
www.howardnaturals.com
Natural cleaners for wood, upholstery, marble, stainless steel, and more.

IKEA
496 West Germantown Pike
Plymouth Meeting, PA 19462
877-345-4532
www.ikea.com
Showroom and mail-order marketer of a wide range of kitchen cabinetry, appliances, and home furnishings. The company is dedicated to removing all hazardous and allergenic materials from its products. It also has strong programs for using sustainable resources and minimizing packaging and waste.

Life Tree
Lotus Brands Inc.
P.O. Box 325
Twin Lakes, WI 53181
800-824-6396
www.lifetreeproducts.com
Offers a complete line of environmentally safe household cleaners, including dish soap, all-purpose cleaners, and laundry liquid. They provide a detailed ingredient list on their Web site.

McHale Landscape Design, Inc.
6212 Leapley Rd.
Upper Marlboro, MD 20772
301-599-8300
www.mchalelandscape.com
Designs, constructs, and plants residential projects, including gardens, arbors, decks, patios, pools, and natural landscapes.

Metro
600 NE Grand Ave.
Portland, OR 97232-2736
503-797-1700
www.metro-region.org
A government Web site for the Portland, Oregon, metropolitan area. It offers information on green cleaners, including the 44-page *Hazardless Home Handbook*.

Miele, Inc.
9 Independence Way
Princeton, NJ 08540
800-843-7231
www.miele.com
Manufactures home appliances, including dishwashers, vacuum cleaners, washing machines, and clothes dryers.

Mohawk Industries, Inc.
160 South Industrial Blvd.
Calhoun, GA 30701
800-266-4295
www.mohawkflooring.com
Manufactures broadloom carpeting, area rugs, hardwood, laminate, ceramic tile, and vinyl flooring. The Mohawk Greenworks Center collects and recycles post-consumer carpets. Mohawk's everSTRAND™ carpet fiber contains 100-percent post-consumer recycled content.

Mothering Magazine

P.O. Box 1690
Santa Fe, NM 87504
505-984-8116
www.mothering.com
An independently owned magazine that addresses contemporary health, personal, environmental, medical, and lifestyle issues. The Web site includes message boards that include discussions of homemade cleaners.

Mountain Rose Herbs

P.O. Box 50220
Eugene, OR 97405
800-879-3337
www.mountainroseherbs.com
Produces and sells certified organic products with a strict emphasis on sustainable agriculture. Products include natural bar soaps, liquid castile soap, and essential oils.

Mrs. Meyer's Clean Day

420 North 5th St., Ste. 600
Minneapolis, MN 55401
877-865-1508
www.mrsmeyers.com
Produces a full line of aromatherapeutic cleaning supplies, including dishwashing powder, shower cleaner, and surface wipes. Cleaning solutions are made with plant-derived ingredients and essential oils. The products don't contain phosphates, chlorine, or harsh solvents.

National Institute for Occupational Safety and Health

395 East St. SW, Ste. 9200
Patriots Plaza Building
Washington, DC 20201
800-232-4636
www.cdc.gov/niosh
The federal agency responsible for conducting research and making recommendations for the prevention of work-related injury and illness. Its Web site includes the *NIOSH Pocket Guide to Chemical Hazards* and is a good source for researching the health risks of a particular chemical.

National Toxicology Program

P.O. Box 12233, MD A3-01
Research Triangle Park, NC 27709
919-541-0530
http://ntp.niehs.nih.gov/
A federal program whose mission is to evaluate agents of public health concern by developing and applying tools of modern toxicology and molecular biology. The NTP is attempting to identify what the effects of the more than 80,000 chemicals registered for use in the United States are and at what levels of exposure they may become hazardous to humans. The program publishes a report every few years that lists chemicals that are confirmed to be carcinogens.

Natural Choices

9525 South 60th St.
Franklin, WI 53132
866-699-2667
www.oxyboost.com
A good source for oxygen-bleach products, as well as a citrus degreaser.

Naturally Yours

1926 South Glenstone Ave. #406
Springfield, MO 65804
888-801-7347
www.naturallyyoursclean.com
Manufactures a complete line of eco-responsible cleaning products, including all-purpose cleaners, degreasers, glass cleaners, mold and mildew removers, tub and tile cleaners, and dishwashing detergents. All products are made with non-toxic ingredients that are biodegradable or naturally degradable.

Optimum Polymer Technologies

P.O. Box 3017
Memphis, TN 38173
901-363-4955
www.optimumcarcare.com
Manufacturers an environmentally friendly car wax that contains no VOCs.

OurHouse

P.O. Box 2327
Danville, IL 61834-23271
877-236-8750
www.ourhouseworks.com
Creates cleaning products that release fewer toxic chemicals, decrease the environmental impact of household cleaning, and use fewer petroleum resources in product formulation, packaging, and transportation. OurHouse products use low-impact agents such as hydrogen peroxide and citrus oil in its products.

Project Laundry List

27 Holly St., Ste. A
Concord, NH 03301
603-226-3098
www.laundrylist.org
A nonprofit organization that focuses on North America's overdependence on unsustainable forms of energy. The company advocates air-drying clothes to conserve energy, and the Web site offers air-drying tips and advice.

The Real Milk Paint Co.

11 West Pumping Station Rd.
Quakertown, PA 18951
800-339-9748
www.realmilkpaint.com
Manufactures nontoxic paints and a citrus solvent that is 98-percent pure citrus peel oil and 2-percent water. It does not contain any emulsions, surfactants, or other additives.

Seaside Naturals

P.O. Box 2097
Short Beach, CT 06405
800-870-1697
www.seasidenaturals.com
Manufactures all-natural cleaning products, including all-purpose cleaners, glass cleaners, floor cleaners, dusting sprays, and bleach alternatives. The family-run company's mission is to educate people on the importance of using nontoxic products in their homes, schools, and workplaces.

Seventh Generation, Inc.

60 Lake St.
Burlington, VT 05401-5218
800-456-1191
www.seventhgeneration.com
Manufactures a leading brand of nontoxic, environmentally safe household products that are available online and in thousands of natural product and grocery stores nationwide, including 100-percent recycled paper towels and biodegradable cleaning, dish, and laundry products. The Web site focuses on answering the questions that consumers frequently ask about household products and their impact on our health and the health of the environment.

Shaklee Corporation

4747 Willow Rd.
Pleasanton, CA 94588
800-SHAKLEE
www.shaklee.com
Manufactures biodegradable household cleaners, including dishwashing concentrate, laundry powder, organic cleaning wipes, microfiber cloths, and spray bottles.

Smithsonian Museum Conservation Institute
4210 Silver Hill Rd.
Suitland, MD 20746
301-238-1240
www.si.edu/mci/
A specialized unit dedicated to research and education in the conservation and preservation of museum collection items and related materials. The MCI offers information on the care and cleaning of antiques.

SoyClean
123 North Orchard
P.O. Box 489
Brooklyn, IA 52211
641-522-9559
www.soyclean.biz
Manufactures a line of nontoxic, soy-bean-based products, including a wood sealer and a paint stripper.

Stacks and Stacks
1045 Hensley St.
Richmond, CA 94801
800-761-5222
www.stacksandstacks.com
Retailer that offers sponges, squeegees, and other cleaning products, along with a great selection of clothes-drying racks (hanging, folding, wall-mounted, and so forth).

Statewide Supply
7352 Darlin Ct.
Dane, WI 53529
800-553-5573
www.statewidesupply.com
The national distributor of Bio-Clean, an environmentally friendly drain cleaner sold directly to plumbing contractors. Bio-Clean only attacks organic waste, such as grease, hair, and food particles, which makes it safe for people, plumbing, and the environment.

TAMKO Building Products, Inc.
EverGrain Composite Decking
Elements Decking
220 West 4th St.
Joplin, MO 64801
800-641-4691
www.tamko.com
www.evergrain.com
www.elementsdecking.com
Manufactures composite decking products using compression molding for a real-wood look.

Teragren
12715 Miller Rd. NE, Ste. 301
Bainbridge Island, WA 98810
800-929-6333
www.teragren.com
Manufactures bamboo flooring, panels, and veneer using environmentally safe materials from rapidly renewable Optimum 5™ Moso bamboo. Teragren is a member of the U.S. Green Building Council.

Trader Joe's
800 South Shamrock Ave.
Monrovia, CA 91016
626-599-3700
www.traderjoes.com
A privately owned and operated food retailer that offers upscale organic and health foods in more than 250 stores in 20 states.

TreeHugger
320 13th St.
Brooklyn, NY 11215
www.treehugger.com
A media outlet dedicated to driving sustainability mainstream. The Web site has green news, solutions, and product information in a variety of formats, including newsletters, tips, forums, blogs, and video segments.

Tried & True Wood Finishes
14 Prospect St.
Trumansburg, NY 14886
607-387-9280
www.triedandtruewoodfinish.com
Manufactures nontoxic linseed oil finishes for wood furniture and countertops. All oil finishes are packaged in recyclable steel cans.

Vermont Soapworks
616 Exchange St.
Middlebury, VT 05753
866-762-7482
www.vermontsoap.com
Manufactures and markets organic, USDA-approved alternatives to chemical- and detergent-based personal care products. Products include handmade bar soaps for sensitive skin, castile liquid soaps, shower gels, pumice stones, pet shampoos, and nontoxic cleaners.

Washington Toxics Coalition
4649 Sunnyside Ave. N, Ste. 540
Seattle, WA 98103
206-632-1545
www.watoxics.org
A nonprofit corporation that protects public health and the environment by eliminating toxic pollution. WTC promotes alternatives, advocates policies, empowers communities, and educates people to create a healthy environment.

Whirlpool Corporation
2000 North M-63
Benton Harbor, MI 49022-2692
800-253-1301
www.whirlpoolcorp.com
Manufactures Energy Star home appliances under the names of Whirlpool, Maytag, KitchenAid, Jenn-Air, Amana, and other brand names.

Whole Foods Market, Inc.
550 Bowie St.
Austin, TX 78703-4644
512-477-4455
www.wholefoodsmarket.com
A retailer of natural and organic foods that also carries an extensive selection of green cleaning products. Whole Foods Market® recently merged with Wild Oats Markets.®

Acid A sour substance with a pH less than 7. It is often used to clean metal objects. Lemon juice and vinegar are examples of mild acids. Acids, which can burn and scar, can be found in toilet-bowl cleaners, metal polishes, and rust removers.

Alkaline Having the properties of an alkali, or base. Examples of cleansers with alkaline properties include baking soda, borax, and washing soda.

Artgum eraser A soft eraser used to rub away pencil marks, greasy spots, and fingerprints on walls and other hard surfaces. Artgum erasers can be purchased at office supply or art supply stores.

Bacteria Microorganisms that typically live in soil, water, organic matter, or the bodies of plants and animals. Certain bacteria are pathogenic for humans.

Baking soda (sodium bicarbonate) A mildly alkaline salt used as an all-purpose cleaner. It's a natural cleanser with an assortment of uses: removes odors, softens water, dissolves dirt and grime, scrubs soap scum, unclogs drains, and more.

Base A bitter substance with a pH greater than 7 that is often used to get rid of food stains and general dirt and grime. Baking soda, borax, and washing soda are examples of mild bases.

Biodegradable Capable of being broken down by living things and absorbed into the ecosystem. A "readily biodegradable" material breaks down in a short period of time.

Borax (sodium borate) A mildly alkaline mineral salt that is useful for removing odors, dissolving dirt, and killing mold and mildew.

Carcinogen A toxic substance that causes or aggravates cancer. Ingredients with carcinogenic properties may be found in typical household cleaning products.

Castile soap A vegetable-oil-based soap that is usually gentler than regular soap and dissolves completely.

Citric acid An acid obtained especially from lemon and lime juices and often found in cleaning products.

Club soda A popular beverage that has sodium citrate, which helps loosen dirt and soften water. Club soda, which is very slightly acidic, is useful for cleaning glass and getting rid of stains.

Compost A mixture that consists of decayed organic matter and is used for fertilizing and improving soil. Also, to convert (as food scraps) to compost.

Concentrated Less diluted. A concentrated liquid or laundry detergent is stronger than detergent that isn't concentrated. A 64-ounce bottle of concentrated laundry detergent, for example, may wash 64 loads while a 64-ounce bottle of a detergent that isn't concentrated may wash only 16 loads.

Condensation The conversion of water from the vapor state to a liquid state, usually initiated by a reduction in temperature of the vapor. The water that forms inside the house—often in the basement—may be caused by air hitting cold windows or pipes dripping.

Detergent A synthetic cleaning product designed to emulsify oils, hold dirt in suspension, and act as a wetting agent. Detergents are usually derived from petroleum products, but they can also be derived from plant oils. Petroleum-based detergents are more harmful to the environment than plant-based detergents.

Disinfectant A cleaning product intended to kill germs, not just remove them. Disinfectants contain hazardous ingredients.

Efflorescence Powdery-white residue that appears on brick and concrete. Efflorescence is caused by water and soluble salts that are trapped behind the wall and are trying to force their way out.

Essential oils Oils used to add scents to cleaning formulas. They may also provide antibacterial qualities. Natural essential oils (made from lemons, peppermint leaves, lavender, and so forth) are safer than artificial fragrances.

Exposure The condition of being subject to some effect. Exposure to certain substances in household cleaning products may trigger a toxic effect.

Fiberboard Wood or vegetable fibers bonded together and compressed into sheets or used as the core for various types of decking.

Global warming An increase in the earth's average atmospheric and oceanic temperatures that is believed to be the result of an increase in the greenhouse effect resulting especially from pollution.

Gray water Household wastewater (from a sink, for example) that does not contain serious contaminants.

Greenhouse gas Gas caused by the greenhouse effect, which is the warming of the surface and atmosphere of the earth that is caused by conversion of solar radiation into heat.

Heartwood The older, nonliving central wood of a tree. Usually darker and denser than younger outer layers of the tree, heartwood sometimes has decay- and insect-resistant properties.

Herbicide An agent used to destroy or inhibit plant growth.

High-efficiency particulate air (HEPA) filters Filters, typically found in vacuums and air-conditioning units, that are designed to remove more than 99 percent of harmful allergens from the air. They help reduce dust, mold spores, pet dander, and other allergens.

Lemon juice A mild acid that is useful in treating alkaline stains (coffee and tea, for example) and cleaning glass.

Medium-density fiberboard (MDF) An engineered product made from compressed wood fibers and used in the construction of furniture and cabinets.

Microfiber A nonabrasive synthetic material (a blend of polyester and polyamide) that removes dust, dirt, and grease from any hard surface, including mirrors, countertops, and computer monitors, without streaking, scratching, or leaving lint. Sharp, wedge-shaped microfibers, many times smaller than a human hair, are constructed to lift, trap, and absorb better than regular fibers, such as cotton. Microfiber, which is machine washable and reusable, absorbs fast and dries quickly.

Mold A superficial growth, produced by fungi, that is prevalent in damp environments (bathrooms and basements, for example). Mildew refers to certain kinds of mold.

Neurotoxin A toxic chemical that has negative effects on the body's brain and nervous system. Quite a few known and suspected neurotoxins are found in cleaning products.

Outgassing Releasing vapors at room temperature. Volatile organic compounds (VOCs) outgas readily and can be harmful to people and the environment.

Oxygen bleach A type of bleach that works by oxidizing and breaking up stains. Gentler and less toxic than chlorine bleach, it is useful for whitening laundry, removing stains from laundry, and cleaning grout.

Particleboard A material composed of wood chips and coarse fibers bonded with adhesive into large sheets. It's commonly used in the fabrication of furniture and countertops.

Pesticide A poisonous chemical solution used to kill ants, spiders, roaches, and other household pests.

Petroleum-based Products, such as certain dish soaps, that are created through a complex, energy-intensive process involving black crude oil that releases toxins into the air. Petroleum-based products are more likely to pose health risks than plant-based products.

pH A measure of acidity and alkalinity of a solution that is a number on a scale (from 0 to 14) on which a value of 7 represents neutrality and lower numbers indicate increasing acidity and higher numbers indicate increasing alkalinity. Each unit of change on the pH scale represents a tenfold change in acidity or alkalinity.

Phosphate A water-softening mineral additive that may be found in automatic dishwashing detergents. Phosphates are

caustic and can be fatal if swallowed.

Plant based Products that are created using natural ingredients derived from plants. Plant-based cleaning products are safer for the environment—and your health—than petroleum-based products.

Polish A cleaning product, used to produce a gloss for the protection and decoration of a surface, that often has toxic ingredients. Many furniture and metal polishes contain hazardous chemicals that are corrosive and may cause eye, skin, or respiratory tract irritation.

Power washer A machine that pumps out high-pressure streams of water and is typically used to clean siding, decks, driveways, and vehicles. Heavy-duty power washers, which are often available for rent, can generate pressures in excess of 3,000 pounds per square inch (PSI).

Pressure-treated (PT) wood Lumber that has had preservative forced into it under pressure to make it decay- and insect-resistant.

Pressure washer See *Power washer*

Pumice stone A tool that is used to remove rust stains or to clean stubborn stains on toilet bowls. Pumice stones can be found at pharmacies in the skin-care section.

PVC A common thermoplastic resin used in a wide variety of products, including spray bottles, flooring, and siding. PVC usually contains toxic chemicals called phthalates and should be avoided.

Saddle soap A mild soap used for cleaning and conditioning leather. Usually used on saddles and bridles, it can be found at tack shops or ordered online.

Sealer A water- or oil-based product used to prevent moisture penetration and its damaging effects.

Sea sponge A natural sponge that can be used as a cleaning tool.

Seepage The quantity of a fluid (often water) that has flowed through fine pours or small openings. Seepage often occurs in basements.

Silver plate Tableware (knives, forks, spoons, and so forth) that is made of silver or a silver-plated base metal. Also, a thin coating of silver on a metallic object.

Squeegee A cleaning tool with a blade (usually rubber) set on a handle that is used for spreading, pushing, or wiping liquid material on, across, or off a surface, such as a window or mirror. Also, to treat with a squeegee.

Stainless steel An alloy of steel with chromium and sometimes another element (such as nickel) that is durable and easy to clean.

Steam cleaner A machine that uses steam to loosen dirt and grime (usually from floors and counters) so it can be vacuumed or wiped off with a clean cloth. Steam cleaners, which use pure water and leave no residue, are available for rent at home centers.

Sump pump A tool used to remove standing water, often in a flooded basement.

Surfactant A surface-active substance, either plant- or petroleum-based, that is the basic ingredient of most laundry and dishwashing detergents. It reduces the surface tension of water so that it can spread more easily over a surface.

Tea tree oil An essential oil from various trees and shrubs of the myrtle family that have aromatic leaves. It is sometimes used as a disinfectant.

Toxin A substance that can cause severe illness, poisoning, disease, or death when ingested, inhaled, or absorbed. Quantities and exposures necessary to cause these effects vary. Many of the chemicals found in household cleaning products have been classified as toxins by the Environmental Protection Agency.

Vinegar A mild acid, typically used for cooking purposes, that is used to neutralize alkaline residues from detergents. Vinegar is an effective natural cleaning product that dissolves soap scum, cleans glass, and disinfects surfaces. It's often used with water to treat stains.

Vinyl A shiny, tough, and flexible plastic that is used especially for flooring, siding, decking, and railing. Also called PVC.

Volatile organic compounds (VOCs) Chemicals containing carbon at a molecular level that easily form vapors and gases at room temperature. Many cleaning products emit VOCs, which can be harmful to people and the environment.

Washing soda (sodium carbonate) A slightly alkaline mineral used as a laundry booster to treat greasy stains and to neutralize odors. It's an effective abrasive cleaner.

Zeolite A mineral with a microporous structure that is often used in water softening. Protect tools from high humidity and moisture (which will cause them to rust) by storing them in a drawer with zeolite to absorb moisture.

Index

A

Acids, 37, 56, 152
Acrylic, 56
Air freshener, 65
Air purifier, 125
Air pollution, 25
Allergy, 32
All-Purpose Liquid Cleaner recipe, 39
All-Surface Spray recipe, 38
Aloe, 37
Aluminum siding, 166
American Association of Poison Control
      Centers, 72
American Lung Association, 30
Appliances, kitchen, 85–86
Artgum eraser, 115
Asphalt roofing, 171
Asthma, 16
Autism, 16

B

Baby laundry, 102
Bacteria, 79, 82
Baking soda, 31–32, 34, 37, 63, 65, 76, 78, 90
Baking Soda Scrub recipe, 44
Bamboo flooring, 130, 140
Bases, 37
Basements, 208–211
      efflorescence, 210
      flood, 209–210
      leaks, 208–209
      mold, 208
      oil tank, 208
      sewage overflow, 211
Bleach alternative, 99
Blinds, 160
Body burden, 16
Body oil, 37
Borax, 34, 37, 63, 89
Broom, 47, 128
Brush, 46, 90
Bucket, 46
Butcher block, 78–79

C

Cabinets, kitchen, 84
Caddy, 47
Candles, 123
Cars, 195–199
      dashboards, 199
      engines, 196
      floors, 199
      seats, 199
      smell, new-car, 196
      undersides, 199
      washing, DIY, 195, 197, 199
      waxes, 198
      windshields and windows, 197
Carpet, 138–145
Carpet shampoo, 140, 142
Carpet sweeper, 138–139
Caulk, 64, 66, 82
Chimney cap, 177
Chrome, 78
Citric acid, 89
Cloth diapers, 105
Clothes-drying rack, 92, 96
Clothing care, 97–98
Cloth rags, 46
Club soda, 37, 145
Concrete floor, 134–137
Consumer Product Safety Commission, 20
Countertop, 76–79
Crude oil, 25–26
Curtains, 160
Cutting board, 78, 82–83

D

Damp mopping, 133–134
Decks
      aluminum, 183
      plywood, 181
      synthetic, 178, 182–183
      wood, 178–182
Dehumidifier, 63
Detergent, 18–19
Dishcloth, 88, 90
Dishwasher, 86–87
Dishwashing liquid, 86
Dishwasher Powder recipe, 41
Dishwashing, versus hand-washing, 89
Disinfectants, 46
Dogs, 128
Drains, clearing, 72–73
Driveways, 186
Dry cleaning, 96
Dry cleaning sponge, 114
Dryer, choosing, 95
Dusting, 122
Dust mop, 48
Dust mopping, 132–133
Dust pan, 47–48, 128

E
Efflorescence, 170, 209–210
Energy Star rating, 59
Entrance mat, 128
Environment, 25, 30
Environmental Protection Agency, 20–21, 30, 79, 159, 169, 206
Essential oils, 32, 36–37, 65

F
Fabric softener, 98–99
Fiberglass, 56, 63
Floor tools, 128–129
Food-prep areas, 79
Forest Stewardship Council, 151, 179
Fungicides, 64

G
Garage floors, 194
Gaskets, 82
Glass, drinking, 88
Glass Cleaner recipe, 40
Global warming, 25
Grade, 176
Grill, 190–191
Grill cover, 190
Grout, 64
Gutters, 175

H
Hair catcher, 54, 73
Hand washables, 102
HEPA filtration, 51, 122
Herbal disinfectant, 79
Herbicides, 26
Hydrochloric acid, 169
Hygrometer, 62

I
Indoor air quality, 30

K
Kitchen exhaust fan, 112
Kitchenware, 86

L
Laundry balls, 102
Laundry detergent, nontoxic, 98–99
Laundry Soap recipe, 42
Lawn clippings, 206
Lawn mowers, 205–206

Leather, 157
Lemon juice, 35, 37, 76
Linoleum, 132
Linseed oil, 78
Liquid soap, 34

M
Marble, 79
Masonry, 168–170
Metal, 120
Metal roofing, 172–173
Metalwork, exterior, 175
Microfiber cloths, 46, 122, 146
Microfiber mop, 128–129, 133
Microwaves, 85
Mildew, 57, 62–67, 167
Mildew and Germ Killer recipe, 43
Mineral deposits, 57
Mirrors, 124
Mold, 57, 62–67
Mop, 48
Moss, 174
Muriatic acid, 169

N
Natural sponges, 46

O
Olive oil, 37, 152
Outdoor fabric, 189
Outdoor furniture, 188–189
Ovens, 85
Oxalic acid, 179
Oxygen bleach, 35, 76, 78, 99

P
Paint
    alternative, 204
    brush, 202–203
    disposal, 204
    spills, 202–203
    thinner, reusing, 204
Patios, masonry, 178
Pesticides, 26, 207
Plant oil, 19
Plastic laminate, 76
Plunger, 72–73
Polish, 152
Porcelain, 56
Pots and pans, 87
Power washing, pros and cons, 168

Pressure washer, 164, 194
Pumice stone, 71

R
Relative humidity, 63, 66
Roofing, 171–175
Roof safety, 173
Rubber broom, 129
Rubber floor, 134–137
Rugs, 138–145
    Snow cleaning, 144
Rust, 37

S
Safety, 36, 73, 173
Scraper, 90–91
Scratches, 151
Shades, 161
Shingle recycling, 172
Shingles, cleaning, 173
Shower curtains, 63
Shower doors, 57
Showerheads, 59
Shower walls, 63
Shutters, 160
Silverware, 90–91
Sinks, 76, 78
Slate roofing, 172
Soap, 18, 34, 37
Soap scum, 37, 56
Soapstone, 136–137
Sodium bicarbonate, 34
Sodium carbonate, 34–35
Sodium percarbonate, 35
Solid surface, 76–77
Splash blocks, 177
Sponges, 79
    disinfecting, 74, 79
Sponge mop, 133
Squeegee, 46, 57, 66, 110–111
Stainless steel, 78
Stains
    carpet, 142, 145
    laundry, 104,
    resistant treatment, 159
    upholstery, 156, 158
    walls, 116
Steam cleaner, 49
Stickers, 151
Stone floor, 134–137
Stoves, 86

Stucco, 170
Surfactant, 18

T
Tabletops, 124, 153–154
Testing, 21–22
Tile, 56, 78
Tile floor, 134–137
Timer, 47, 67, 69
Toilet-bowl cleaners, 70
Toilet brush, 70
Toilets, 70–71
Toxic Substances Control Act, 20
Trash pullout, 88

U
Upholstery, 155–158
U.S. Department of Energy, 84

V
Vacuum, 50–51
Veneers, 153
Venting fan, 62–63, 67–69
Vinegar, 35, 37, 56, 62, 65, 67, 76, 133, 152
Vinyl floor, 134–137
Vinyl siding, 166
Volatile organic compounds, 24, 26

W
Walls, 112–116
Washing machine, choosing, 95
Washing soda, 34–35, 37, 63
Water conservation, 59
Water pollution, 26, 29
Water spots, 37
Wax, 150, 152
Wet mopping, 135
Wicker, 154
Windows, 108–111
Window treatments, 159–161
Windshields, 197
Wood decks
    cleaning, 181–182
    maintaining, 180
    protecting, 181
Wood floors, 132–133
Wood furniture, 148–152
    problems 151
Wood roofing, 171–172
Wood siding, 166
Workshop tools, 200–201

Have a home improvement, decorating, or gardening project? Look for these and other fine

Creative Homeowner books

wherever books are sold.

500 color photos. 224 pp.; 8½"x10⅞"
$ 19.95 (US) $ 24.95 (CAN)
BOOK #: 279415

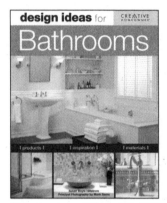

500 color photos. 224 pp.; 8½"x10⅞"
$ 19.95 (US) $ 24.95 (CAN)
BOOK #: 279268

275 color photos. 256 pp.; 9¼"x10⅞"
$ 21.95 (US) $ 25.95 (CAN)
BOOK #: 279031

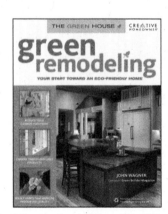

300 color photos. 208 pp.; 8½"x10⅞"
$ 19.95 (US) $ 22.95 (CAN)
BOOK #: 279053

For more information and to order directly, go to
www.creativehomeowner.com